HEART
ON MY
SLEEVE

Stories from a Life Well Worn

JEANNE BEKER

Foreword by Linda Evangelista

PUBLISHED BY SIMON & SCHUSTER

New York | London | Toronto | Sydney | New Delhi

A Division of Simon & Schuster, LLC
166 King Street East, Suite 300
Toronto, Ontario M5A 1J3

This Simon & Schuster Canada edition October 2024

Simon & Schuster: Celebrating 100 Years of Publishing in 2024

For information about special discounts for bulk purchases,
please contact Simon & Schuster Special Sales at 1-800-268-3216
or CustomerService @simonandschuster.ca.

Interior design by Joy O'Meara
Illustrations by Bekky O'Neil

Manufactured in the United States of America

1   3   5   7   9   10   8   6   4   2

Library and Archives Canada Cataloguing in Publication

Title: Heart on my sleeve : stories from a life well worn / by Jeanne Beker.
Names: Beker, Jeanne, author.
Description: Simon & Schuster Canada edition.
Identifiers: Canadiana (print) 20240304640 | Canadiana (ebook) 20240341104 |
ISBN 9781668035207 (hardcover) | ISBN 9781668035214 (EPUB)
Subjects: LCSH: Beker, Jeanne. | LCSH: Journalists—Canada—Biography. |
LCSH: Fashion. | LCGFT: Autobiographies.
Classification: LCC TT505.B44 A3 2024 | DDC 746.9/2092—dc23

ISBN 978-1-6680-3520-7
ISBN 978-1-6680-3521-4 (ebook)

*For Marilyn, who first turned me on to all things cool . . .
and for Iain, who trusted in the magic of the moonlight.*

CONTENTS

CONTENTS

HEART
ON MY
SLEEVE

FOREWORD

When Jeanne asked me if I might consider writing this foreword, I said yes . . . and then immediately regretted it! I'm a model, not a writer. But then I realized that Jeanne and I are fellow Canadians who have both been obsessed with fashion from an early age, and whose love of fashion helped build a career around it—and the thought of writing this became less intimidating. Let me just say up front that I'll never remember what year or where it was when we first met—because, unlike Jeanne, who has a crystal-clear memory—my recall isn't so good. However, I'm going to venture that our first meeting was most likely backstage at a fashion show. Which one and where? You'll have to ask her! But it only makes sense that we would have met at a show. After all, we were two Ontarians making our mark in the world of fashion.

The backstage area at any given fashion show in the late eighties and early nineties was like no place that had ever existed before and probably never will again. No one had an entourage, and none of the models were celebrities—at least not at first. And since there were no mobile phones or social media to distract anyone, there was only the steady chatter of hundreds of voices all speaking, laughing, or shouting at once, gossiping and sharing confidences while a soundtrack of the latest chart-toppers blasted in the background. From Paris to Milan, London to New York, models—along with a cast of hairstylists, makeup artists, fashion editors, photographers, and journalists—formed a kind of traveling circus: All of us knew one another, as we had gone to the same parties and dinners, gone to the same shows, and been on the same flights to the next destination. In short, we were a tribe of fashion vagabonds.

Amidst all of this was Jeanne, who would appear backstage, wide-eyed and smiling, greeting everyone with a "How are you doing?" She always spoke with the warmth of someone who actually wanted to *know* how you were doing, and she was the first journalist who asked models what *we* thought! Not only about the shows we were in but about our takes on hair and makeup trends and street style. You name it, she asked . . . and we always answered. Through her show *Fashion Television*, Jeanne was able to bring not only the looks from runway shows but the energy and irresistible chaos of the backstage into living rooms across the globe. She managed to change the way ordinary people thought about the fashion world—and she made fashion accessible. As a result, many of us industry workers—including Jeanne—became household names, something none of us had ever imagined.

One of the most endearing and relatable things about Jeanne is that—as for most of us in the industry—her love affair with fashion began at an early age and never diminished. Like her, most of us can't explain *why* we loved it—we just knew that we had to be part of it. And our love of fashion began in small ways—with a favorite blue denim jumpsuit that was worn in almost every photo taken during the sixth grade, or a knit cape made by a beloved grandmother that was the best birthday gift ever. Jeanne's love of fashion, like my own, is rooted in how a piece made us *feel* and in the memory of that feeling. These personal connections are so important in understanding our feelings about what we wear, and I think everyone—even if they're not part of the fashion world—can relate to that.

As you read this book, you'll see that the beauty of Jeanne's storytelling—and I say *storytelling,* because I believe storytelling is a gift, while writing is a skill—is that it's rooted in the lives of her parents, who shared their incredible stories with her, inspiring her to see and experience the world in her own unique way. Now, Jeanne can tell all of us what her journey has been like.

Fashion often gets a bad rap for being vapid and frivolous, considering how many crushing conflicts and struggles plague our world. However, I've always found that the magic of fashion is its power to bring us together—no matter what culture or background or socioeconomic group we come from. Fashion, and how we use it, is a commentary on who we are at certain moments in our lives, on how we see ourselves and how we want to be seen. *Heart on My Sleeve* invites us to recall our own lives and defining moments—where we were, what we wore, and how we felt. I can't think of a better inspiration for those memories than my dear Jeanne.

Linda Evangelista
New York City
January 2024

INTRODUCTION

A Wardrobe of Memory

Clothing is . . . an exercise in memory.
It makes me explore the past: how did I feel when I wore that.
[Clothes] are like signposts in the search for the past . . .

LOUISE BOURGEOIS

From a very young age, I was acutely aware of fashion's transformational powers. My earliest memories are of playing with paper dolls. *McCall's*, a popular American magazine back in the 1950s, featured a monthly cutout doll named Betsy along with a page full of her pretty party dresses. My big sister and my mother would cut out all those fantastic garments, and we'd dress Betsy to suit whatever mood we thought she was in—or rather, whatever mood we were in at the time. Later came fancier paper dolls—complete books featuring various movie and TV stars of the era, and their ultraglam outfits, which would dictate more grown-up, exciting adventures. Dressing those glamorous cardboard gals would keep my sister and me occupied for hours.

When Barbie arrived on the scene in 1959, I was desperate to have her, but my parents had just purchased their suburban dream bungalow and were counting their pennies. So instead of Barbie, I got her knockoff, Mitzi, a cheap and tawdry version of the A-list doll. I was determined to glam her up as best I could, and thanks to my mother's patience with a sewing machine, we concocted a dream wardrobe for Mitzi—one that lifted her to new fashion heights. In the end, Mitzi outshone my friends' real Barbies, and all of them coveted her spectacular one-of-a-kind wardrobe. Mitzi taught me the power of original style and the importance of self-expression through wardrobe.

As I grew older and my own clothing stash blossomed, I always treasured pieces that made me feel special or confident. All through my teens, my crafty mum made most of my clothing—terrific mod-inspired garments that never failed to garner attention. By the time my TV career started to take off in the eighties, first covering the music scene and then fashion, I had access to an impressive array of designer wares. I began to understand how vitally important it was to develop style consistency, a look that would not only define my image but allow me to express myself in bold and striking ways.

Now, after a lifetime spent playing dress-up, I understand fashion's power more than ever. The clothing and accessories we choose to wear are emblematic of who we are at key points in time. What we wear not only serves to elevate and transform us but also triggers memories of moments we hold dear. Clothing provides snapshots of the past, revealing how we want others to see us and how we want to see ourselves.

Most women can relate to the excitement of fashion, but my entire life has been steeped in it, personally and professionally. For the three decades known as fashion's "Golden Age," I was wildly fortunate to have a ringside seat. I attended the world's most famous designer shows, covering them as a host and segment producer for the internationally syndicated series *Fashion Television*.

My unprecedented backstage access allowed me to get up-close and personal with some of the greatest creative minds of our time. And all the while, I was given an extraordinary education on the subject of style. I got to learn from the great Valentino, who lamented the fact that fashion's countless options had become so dizzying for women that "they no longer know on which foot to dance." Then there was the legendary Bill Blass, who believed that "women who dress in the same designer fare from head to toe are a crashing bore."

At fashion shows around the globe, I would sit alongside famous style icons like André Leon Talley, Daphne Guinness, and Isabella Blow—all larger-than-life fashionistas who'd mastered the art of dressing. They made me look at my own humble wardrobe in fresh new ways. But more important, I grew to appreciate the backstories of pieces of clothing and accessories, and I gained a new reverence for fashion's possibilities.

In the pages of this book, my wardrobe becomes the catalyst for stories about my life. I walk you through memories of jewelry, accessories, and pieces of clothing that have earned indelible places in my mind—because that's what really great fashion does: It creates a feeling that lasts forever; it creates a mood that transcends time.

Through these stories, you'll walk a mile in my shoes and get a feel for the memorable outfits I once wore. You'll meet my family and some of my friends who in so many ways, small and large, inspired my life in fashion. You'll also meet the great fashion and music stars who made an impact on my wardrobe and, more important, on me.

My hope is that this book inspires you to look at your own wardrobe in a whole new way, for what is fashion if not an entry point to stories about who we are and how we want to be remembered? The clothes and accessories we choose to wear say so much about us and act as valuable touchstones, reminding us of how far we've come.

In her book *Dressed: A Philosophy of Clothes,* Shahidha Bari refers to items of clothing as the "wordless witnesses to our lives." Indeed, our personal garments and accessories offer precious glimpses of our inner selves, far beyond what a mirror could ever reflect. And while clothes do serve practical and perfunctory purposes, the special pieces we hold on to are often keys to treasured memories. Even when we can't actually hang on to our old outfits, the memories of them—and of our past selves—remain.

Please enjoy this intimate look into my walk-in closet of fashion memories. I hope you'll find pieces that resonate with you, that you like, recognize, or remember. Moreover, I hope that through my telling of these personal stories, you'll see how the best outfit of all is a well-worn life.

A Satchel of Discovery

The simplest wardrobe accoutrements can sometimes resonate the loudest. The worn old satchel that lived at the back of my mother's bedroom closet for years was a far cry from the glamorous fashion accessories that would one day become so commonplace in my life. But there was a distinct, precious quality to this bag—a kind of gravitas—that was never lost on me, even as a young child. While the humble old satchel is now lost to time, and I never got to use it myself, the reverence I always had for it is unparalleled: It represented my family's history to me, and what could be more precious than that?

My mother brought the brown leather satchel with her when she came to Canada from Austria in 1948. It was stuffed with precious old black-and-white photos of relatives, most of whom had perished in the Holocaust, some of whom had survived and found refuge at Bindermichl, the Austrian displaced persons camp where my parents lived for three years after the war.

Miraculously, my parents survived the horrors of the Holocaust, thanks in part to their wits and to the kindness of strangers. My dad was a soldier in the Polish army, while my mum was an idealistic, intellectual student, seven years younger than my dad. They both came from the same place—a small village called Kozowa in what was then eastern Poland. They met on a blind date, fell deeply in love, and carried on a clandestine relationship. My mother's father was a very religious man and would never have approved of my dad. After all, he was that much older than my mother and from a very poor family on the wrong side of the tracks. My mother was eighteen years old when the war broke out, and when the Nazis arrived in her shtetl, she and nine of her family members hid in a secret underground bunker in her father's house. While trying to locate the bunker, the Nazis plugged up some pipes through which my mother and her relatives were getting air. All of her family suffocated right in their own home. My mother was the sole survivor.

Shortly thereafter, my father, realizing that it was only a matter of time before the Germans captured and killed him for being a Jew, deserted the army and made his way back to Kozowa to look for my mother. They reunited and together went into hiding—in barns, cellars, and attics. At one point, they spent three months in a dark hole underground. They were constantly on the run, knowing that at any moment they could be discovered and killed.

These were the dark stories I grew up hearing. My parents

talked about their wartime experiences incessantly, as a form of therapy, I suppose. When I was younger, it was frightening to hear their tales. Yet I was incredibly proud of my amazing parents, who'd managed not only to survive but to rebuild their shattered lives. They had the courage to immigrate to a new country where they knew no one and couldn't even speak the language. Their resilience always impressed me, and it still does to this day.

To me, my mum and dad were superhuman, and even though I was sometimes embarrassed by the fact that they spoke English with an accent, I inherently knew that they possessed rare toughness and tenacity. I also knew they'd given up so much for my sister and me to grow up in a great, free country where dreams could be realized if you worked hard enough.

"Don't be afraid," my dad always used to tell us. "And never give up!" This attitude had gotten him and my mother through the war.

"It's not so easy to live a life," my mother used to say with her trademark sigh—such a different statement from my dad's. She was a great sentimentalist, and I know that as much as she tried to live in the present, a big part of her was stuck in the past, surrounded by the ones she had loved and lost.

For me, that old brown satchel *was* my family history. Transported to Canada via ocean liner in a big wooden chest, that bag was the only connection to a life my mother missed so desperately and I would never know. The photos contained in that old leather bag were the ultimate treasure trove: memories of relatives my mother would describe to me as though they were alive and about to walk through the front door.

I regarded that satchel as forbidden fruit. I wasn't really permitted to look at it on my own. But when I was seven, we moved into a new house in the suburbs, and I was delighted to discover the old bag hiding at the back of my parents' bedroom closet. On a mission to discover my roots, I spent hours quietly sitting on the floor of that little closet, secretly studying those old images, savoring the proof that, once upon a time, my family was more like other kids' families, with lots of aunts and uncles and cousins and even grandparents.

But my mother would never leave me alone with those treasures for very long.

"Are you looking at those old pictures again? You have to be careful with them," she'd say over and over. "Nothing lasts forever."

Even at my tender age, I knew what she meant. She was referring to her idyllic prewar life in the old country, trying to rationalize how so many of the beloved people in her life were no longer alive. I was always acutely aware of just how much loss both my parents had suffered.

As I perused those photos, I remember wondering: Will this ancient satchel last forever? What if it doesn't? And what will become of my mother's precious photo collection should its container fall to pieces? And what if the photos themselves don't last forever? What would that do to my mother?

There was one large family portrait that was the most impressive photograph of the lot, taken in 1938, about a year before the war. It featured my mum as a lovely seventeen-year-old, and her strikingly beautiful sister Sarah, who was only about a year older than my mum was. They stood behind my grandparents, who both looked rather stern. My grandfather had a long white beard, as most orthodox Jews did at the time, and my grandmother was a stout, frowning woman. She didn't look very happy, but my mum always told me she was loving and kind.

There was a handful of well-dressed men and women standing around them—my mum's half brothers and their wives—and a group of assorted children sitting on the ground, the kinds of young cousins I always wished I had. No one in the photo was smiling at all. *Why should they,* I reckoned, *with a horrible fate about to befall them?* There were also photos of my mother and father postwar, in the DP camp, looking like forties movie stars—a gorgeous couple, true survivors filled with optimism, getting ready for their next big adventure.

That satchel, as weathered and plain as it was, always gave me a feeling of comfort and warmth, a sense of connection and belonging. I'd sometimes sling it over my shoulder and pose in front of the closet door mirror, admiring how grown up and important it made me look, knowing how valuable its contents were to our lives. But just like my mother always said, nothing lasts forever. I don't know exactly what happened to that bag, but eventually it must have fallen apart and been thrown away. Those precious photos, however, remained intact, finding safe haven in containers, albums, frames, and drawers in my home and in the homes of my family members.

I often think of that worn old satchel as the first accessory that really meant something to me, and even though it no longer exists, I recall it with fondness. And I'm grateful to it for doing what it was meant to do—delivering those photos safely through wars and conflicts, across oceans and countries, making sure that my family, the ones who didn't make it, are remembered to this day.

When the Slipper Fits

When my parents arrived in Canada, they scrimped and saved to buy a house of their own. Then, in 1952, the year I was born, my father, hell-bent on being an independent businessman, started a small slipper factory in our basement. Little did I know this basement business would be my first foray into the dynamic world of the garment industry.

My dad and his partner, Eli Skorecki, a fellow Holocaust survivor, met while briefly working at another slipper factory in downtown Toronto. Wanting to be their own bosses, they felt they'd learned enough to start their own enterprise. They invested in a small machine designed for sewing plush fabrics, and they decided to make children's novelty slippers—whimsical offerings that featured bunny, kitten, tiger, and clown heads, complete with plastic googly eyes and felt noses. They even put little squeakers in the heads to make them more appealing to kids.

After creating a mini collection, my dad and Skorecki (as my dad always called Eli) started pitching their wares to a variety of Canadian retailers, from the Bata Shoe Company to Woolworth's, Eaton's, and Simpson's. Once they'd collected orders, they rented a factory space downtown in Toronto's garment district and launched Quality Slippers and Vest Manufacturing Co. Ltd. They'd also begun making men's sheepskin vests.

As a child, I was terribly proud of my dad for being at the helm of this buzzing little business. It was very important for him, since he abhorred the idea of working for someone else. He had an incredible work ethic and often toiled at "the shop," as he called it, seven days a week, twelve hours a day. I'd regularly visit him there after my piano lessons every Saturday afternoon.

I remember walking through the doors of that old, dilapidated factory and the comforting scent that would hit me—a cross between the sheepskin and the leather. It was like entering a living snow globe, because tiny fibers floated fantastically in the air, the result of all the plush fabric being used. My dad's face lit up from across the floor the moment he spotted me, which made the whole place all the more magical. He'd immediately get up from the little machine he worked at and head right for me, throwing his arms open to receive a giant hug. Then he'd walk me around the factory, showing me off to all his wonderful, devoted workers.

Waiting for my dad to wrap up work, I'd hang out in his office, which felt especially important. The walls were lined with shelves featuring countless sample slippers, some made right in the factory and others made in Japan. My dad used these overseas samples as inspiration, and I'm sure there were a few styles he managed to knock off. In those days, Japan provided the biggest competition for a Canadian independent manufacturer like my dad, who was tormented by the fact that the Japanese product could be made so much more economically than he could manage.

Dad was always trying to undercut the prices of his competitors, even by a cent or two, just so he could get more orders. By watching my dad and that factory operate, I got a real sense from an early age of what the business of fashion was all about. How do you keep coming up with novel ideas season after season? How do you control your manufacturing and make sure you have good people on your team? How do you find the best materials at the best prices? How do you not only keep up with the competition but surpass them?

I learned by watching my dad just how hard a fashion entrepreneur has to work to keep the wolf at bay. While he never did manage to make millions from his little business, he put a roof over our heads and afforded our family a comfortable lifestyle. Somehow, through grit and determination, he made ends meet. Little did he know that his young daughter would eventually, in her own unique way, enter the fashion industry, following in his footsteps—or rather, in his plush slippers.

Resurrection

As much as I've always appreciated and adored vintage clothing, I personally never collected or even wore much of it. You need an unabashed confidence to style and strut it properly, and I lacked that bravado when I was younger. But I do especially treasure one fancy seventies frock in my wardrobe—an elegant sea green and gold lace confection that my mother had custom-made and had proudly worn to many dressy affairs back in her day.

My mum was a great lover of fashion to the day she died. She had subscriptions to both *Vogue* and *Harper's Bazaar*. When I was young, she, my sister, and I would spend hours poring over the pages of aspirational glossy magazines, dreaming about our favorite looks and scheming about ways we could replicate them.

"Ooooh! I love the A-line of that dress," my sister, Marilyn, piped up as she spotted one especially mod creation. "And those bell sleeves. Wouldn't it look cool if it was made out of that crazy zebra corduroy material Mummy just bought?"

"That could be really nice," my mum concurred.

"And I could wear it with my white go-go boots! That would be so perfect!" said Marilyn.

My eleven-year-old self delighted in hearing Marilyn's lofty fashion ideas, and in my mum's willingness to try just about anything. While we could never afford to purchase any designer labels, my mother took up sewing in the sixties with great zeal, and she whipped up some fabulous fare for herself and for my sister and me, too.

But when it came to evening dresses, Mum didn't necessarily trust her own abilities. Special-occasion wear she'd have custom-made: first, by an Italian dressmaker and later, by a German woman named Mrs. Olson.

Mrs. Olson was a remarkably skilled seamstress. She lived just outside of Toronto in a suburb called King City, and a trip to her house meant there was a grand occasion coming up in our family. We had to look our best, and my mum was determined to see to it that we did.

Of course, before we'd trek out to King City to meet with Mrs. Olson, my mum would search Stitsky's, the grand fabric emporium downtown, for fabrics and notions for our impending couture creations.

Still, no trip to King City was complete without Fela Jaskolka, one of my mother's best friends. The ever-stylish Mrs. Jaskolka, a humble grocer's wife, lived around the corner from us. My mother considered her a grand maven of good taste. After buying fabrics or even clothes we liked, we often ran around the corner to get

Mrs. Jaskolka's opinion, and even though my mother herself was the ultimate connoisseur, if Mrs. Jaskolka really liked what we'd chosen, we knew we were onto something good. Furthermore, if Mrs. Jaskolka really *chalished* (Yiddish for "fainted") over our choices, we knew we had the makings of a showstopping outfit. Of course, if Mrs. Jaskolka merely sniffed, that meant returning our finds from wherever we got them and starting from scratch again.

Sometimes, Mrs. Jaskolka would visit our house for approval, too. I'll never forget hearing the doorbell, then opening the door to find the statuesque Mrs. Jaskolka standing on our stoop, modeling some swank ensemble.

"So, Jeannala. Vat do you tink?" she would ask in her thick Polish accent, a huge grin on her face.

"Oh, it's so nice!" I'd say. "Mum! Come to the door. Mrs. Jaskolka's here, and she looks amazing!"

As soon as my mum came into the vestibule, she'd invite Mrs. Jaskolka inside, and the two of them would preen and pose in our front hall mirror, my mother adjusting her friend's "ja-*ket*," as she called it, or tilting her fedora just so.

This dynamic duo of chic regularly went together to Stitsky's, returning with heaps of extraspecial goods—sumptuous materials that sent their couture fantasies soaring.

"Oy, this is gonna be something," my mum declared as she spread yards of gorgeous lace on her bed one afternoon.

"It's gonna look a million dollars!" piped in Mrs. Jaskolka.

"And it's French!" Mum added, inspecting the pale green-and-gold fabric more closely. "I'm taking it to Mrs. Olson tomorrow morning. We're going to make a gown!"

Within a couple of weeks, my mum's fantasy had come to life, and she was twirling in front of her bedroom mirror, delighted with her latest fashion statement. The simply cut green-and-gold lace gown became one of her favorites, and she got a lot of good use out of it, sporting it at a whole range of joyous celebrations.

Fast-forward to 2005. My mum was purging her closets for an impending move. She came across her precious creation and held it up for me to admire.

"Such a beautiful dress, isn't it?" she said, her eyes misting over as the memories came rushing back. "Maybe Bekky or Joey will want to wear it one day? We could alter it a bit, and I bet it'll fit both of them perfectly," she said.

My diminutive mum was a good six or seven inches shorter than my girls, and a bit more *zaftig* than my slender daughters, too, so I wasn't convinced this gown would ever really fit either of them properly, but regardless, I found myself saying, "Sure, Mum. I'll keep the dress for them."

I could tell she was greatly relieved, that she wanted this special piece to stay in the family even if it never got worn again.

A few weeks later, a fashion crisis reared its head: I had a swish black-tie Bar Mitzvah to attend, and nothing to wear. I searched my closet desperately, to the point that it looked like a tsunami had hit my room. I was about to give up when Mum's green-and-gold lace dress came into view.

Hmm, I thought. *Dare I try it on?* My mum was quite a bit rounder than I was, but maybe there was a way to make it work? What did I have to lose?

I pulled away the plastic wrapping and took the dress off the hanger. I stepped into the gown and eyed myself in the mirror. Wow, what a beautiful piece of work this was! I was impressed by the painstaking construction—the details hand-stitched, and the entire dress lined with satin. But most impressive of all was that the gown fit me so perfectly, though it was only cocktail length on me, rather than being a full-length gown. I was beyond delighted with the way it looked—and the way it made me feel, too.

There was an air of authentic luxury to this garment. It was not just another little cocktail frock that could be purchased at any high-end boutique. No, this dress was unique, bespoke, a true-blue vintage piece, which was very on trend. It had originated from the imagination of my mum, Mrs. Jaskolka, and the German dressmaker, Mrs. Olson, who had sewn it. More than that, this was a gown with a story.

I put it on for that big event and teamed it with a pair of gold Manolo strappy heels, rhinestone vintage earrings, and a matching bracelet. Va-va-voom!

Once dressed, I picked up the phone to call my mum. "Ma, you'll never guess what I'm wearing to that Bar Mitzvah tonight!"

"What?" she asked. "I know there'll be a lot of fancy people there. I hope it's not just another little black dress again."

"No! Your green-and-gold lace gown!"

"Oy, really?" she kvelled. "I can't believe it!"

I could tell she was happy. The torch had been passed, and I had reinforced my mum's firm belief that she and Mrs. Jaskolka were bona fide fashion mavens ahead of their time.

The Bar Mitzvah, held at the swank Four Seasons Hotel, was a splashy affair, and all the women who attended were swathed in high-end designer finery. They looked as though they'd stepped out of the pages of *Vogue*. And then there was me, in my mum's thirty-five-year-old homemade gown. Was I embarrassed? Far from it. I was crazy proud!

"Your dress is so gorgeous, Jeanne!" the fashionistas all gushed when they saw me. And with every compliment, I replied, "It's vintage, my mother's creation. She has quite the eye, you know."

The only downside to wearing the dress was that it was a very hot evening, and I was roasting. The woman seated next to me noted my situation: "The trouble with this vintage stuff is that it doesn't breathe."

Nonetheless, as steamy as I felt, I got on the dance floor after dinner.

As I danced the hora with my two beautiful daughters, I remembered that old adage—how we all turn into our mothers at some point. I thought about how many horas the dress I was wearing had seen in its day, and about all those years it had hung at the back of my mum's closet, patiently waiting to be resurrected. My younger, mod-hippie self would never have seen this coming, but suddenly my heart was filled with untold joy as I danced in my mum's old dress, experiencing all the happiness it undoubtedly had given her.

Popping Pom-Poms

My first brush with rock greatness involved a yellow bikini top with black pom-poms. I was attending the 1969 Toronto Pop Festival with my friend Esther Goldfluss, and I was seventeen years old.

In an effort to dress as cool and as sexy as possible, I paired the attention-getting top with a low-slung, hip-hugging pair of faded denim bell-bottoms. For modesty's sake, I wore a big yellow shirt over the whole outfit, tied at the waist. The sassy getup was so empowering: I was ready to boogie it up at this groundbreaking festival, which predated Woodstock.

By midday Varsity Stadium was rocking with a fabulous lineup, including a rather frenetic set by Arkansas-born rockabilly legend Ronnie Hawkins. Just to keep us all on our toes, one of our friends had been passing out caffeine tablets called "Wake Up" pills—the perfect pick-me-up after all the weed we'd been smoking that morning.

When Ronnie and his band launched into "Hey! Bo Diddley," I got up and started dancing my butt off. I didn't hold back. We were in a prime location, right in front of the stage, and no doubt because I was wearing bright yellow, Ronnie quickly spotted me in the crowd and began motioning for me to come up on stage with him.

"Me?" I mouthed, almost certain he must be pointing to someone else, but when he nodded and beckoned to me again, I realized he was really and truly talking to me.

"What are you waiting for? Get up there!" Esther said. She'd been watching all of this go down, and now she pushed me forward, and a big cop who was stationed in front of the stage helped lift me right up next to Ronnie himself.

Once I was up there, I figured this was my big chance to be "discovered." I brazenly took off my big yellow shirt to flaunt my yellow pom-pom bikini top underneath. That's when I started shaking it as though my life depended on it.

It felt like the crowd of 60,000 definitely approved, and for the next few minutes, I was living a teenage dream of the highest order. Ronnie seemed thrilled that he had plucked this eager little dancing queen from the crowd. He flashed several big smiles at me as I boogied on his stage.

When the song ended, I was helped off the platform and a photographer who'd been snapping pics asked for my name and address. *Well, all right,* I thought. *I really have arrived!*

The next day, my mother got a call from her friend Mrs. Kreinick. "Do you realize," Mrs. Kreinick said, "that your little Jeanne, dressed in something very skimpy, is on the front page of *The Toronto Telegram*'s entertainment section?"

"What are you talking about?" my mother demanded. "My Jeanne?"

My mother called me into the kitchen and quizzed me about what she'd heard.

"Well, yeah, Mummy," I sheepishly replied. "I did get asked up onstage and I danced for a few minutes. And, uhhh, yeah. I was wearing my jeans and a bikini top," I said as though this sort of thing happened every day.

My mother's face said it all. She was not amused.

"Mum, it was really hot out! A lot of the girls were wearing bikini tops!"

My poor mother. She rolled her eyes and didn't say a word.

Later that afternoon, the newspaper boy delivered the paper to our door. Seeing the layout of photos of me in rock critic Peter Goddard's cool "After Four" column was nothing short of dizzying. The caption read: "Fan Jeanne Beker, 17, of Faywood Blvd., couldn't resist the Ronnie Hawkins beat and was invited onstage for an impromptu dance."

My parents were outraged, and as thrilled as I was to have made the paper, I was a tad mortified that they'd actually *printed* my home address as part of the piece. Now the weirdos would know where to find me . . . though they'd have to reckon with my parents if they had the nerve to come to the door!

A day later, I got a call from a guy named Heavy Andrews,

Ronnie Hawkins's manager, saying that he and Ronnie wanted to meet "that chick" who'd given them all such great publicity. Once again, I was certain that I'd made it! I put on a tight little dress and heels and headed downtown to the band's offices in the Hawk's Nest, upstairs from the hip Le Coq d'Or nightclub.

Heavy Andrews, an avuncular character with a big white beard and twinkling blue eyes, was sitting behind a huge desk when I entered. It seemed that he called everybody "Baby Blue." He introduced me to Ronnie as "Baby Blue," and together, he and Ronnie started telling me about another cool rock festival that was taking place later that summer in upstate New York. They were still trying to get Ronnie on the bill, but if they could, would I be interested in doing another "impromptu" dance onstage with the band? They would have me dropped out of a helicopter as soon as Ronnie started singing "Hey! Bo Diddley."

"Only this time, Baby Blue," Heavy went on to say, "we want you to take off your bikini top!"

While it was an outrageously creepy proposition, it was the kind of lewd idea that, sadly, was in keeping with the times. The musical *Hair* had debuted on Broadway just a year before, and public nudity was considered by many to be a show of liberation rather than a form of exploitation.

Although I was tempted to entertain Heavy's proposal— especially since Ronnie also promised that should I accept the offer, he'd take me to visit his old pal Elvis Presley in Memphis (swoon!)—I knew my mother would never stand for it. I told Heavy and Ronnie that I'd have to think about it, but I knew me going topless at that show was simply not happening.

The festival they were talking about turned out to be the famed Woodstock. But sadly, Ronnie didn't get that gig. Maybe he would've, though, if he'd promised a spirited topless dancer as part of the act!

Years later, after Elvis died, when I was hosting *The New-Music,* I went to Memphis to interview Ronnie Hawkins about his early roots. We visited Sun Studio, where he'd recorded in the fifties, and then we went to Graceland, where I'd arranged for a private tour. We sat in Elvis's famous TV room, and Ronnie was thrilled—although he sheepishly confessed he'd never gotten along with Elvis. That's the way it is sometimes. Showbiz is part mythology and part smoke and mirrors. Some people will say anything to help fuel the magic.

The year after my first Ronnie Hawkins encounter, in the summer of 1970—wearing a trendy, hand-embroidered peasant shirt—I made the trek to Centre Island with my high school pal Itzy Bornstein for the legendary annual Mariposa Folk Festival. With artists like Joni Mitchell and Ramblin' Jack Elliott on the bill, I figured the weekend extravaganza was *the* place to be, and I was pumped to learn more about the heady folk scene.

The musicians were performing under large tents, and the very first one we wandered into was alive with the Cajun fiddling of Doug Kershaw, a Louisiana sensation who was burning up the place with a mean version of "Orange Blossom Special."

Doug was a wiry little guy with huge muttonchops and shaggy dark hair, clad in an emerald-green velvet suit, and I was mesmerized by his sheer energy and frenzied style. I was standing at the back of the tent, but somehow, I caught his eye and immediately knew by the look on his face that he wanted to make contact. So when his impressive show was over and Itzy headed to the next tent, I stayed behind to see if I could indeed meet this Bayou wonder.

After a few minutes of greeting friends and fans, Doug made a beeline for me. "Well, hello, you pretty thing!" he said, in his deep southern drawl.

We made a little small talk, and he asked me if I was at the festival alone. I told him I'd come with a friend, but we were each doing our own thing at the moment.

"How about we meet back here at five and we return to the city together?" he suggested. I was thoroughly charmed and up for the adventure. I agreed to the plan, knowing Itzy would understand.

Doug and I took the ferryboat back to downtown Toronto, numerous fans trying to chat him up all the way. I was fascinated by how everybody was fawning over him and impressed by how kind he was and how unaffected he seemed by all the attention.

When we got to the Toronto ferry dock, Doug suggested we go to his hotel room so he could freshen up before taking me to dinner. Part of me thought I must be crazy to be going to a musician's hotel room—especially with a musician I'd just met! But another part of me felt so grown-up and cool. I could handle whatever weirdness might crop up, right? And who could resist this up close and personal encounter with such an incredible talent?

We took a cab to the old Four Seasons Motor Hotel on Jarvis Street, where all the Mariposa musicians were staying, and we went up to Doug's room. Somehow, the small room seemed a little sad to me, terribly unglamorous, with a big stand-up steamer trunk in the middle. "That's where I keep all my costumes," Doug told me. "Wanna see 'em?"

Of course I was game, so he opened the trunk to reveal a dazzling display of tailored and colorful jackets, many in plush brocades, with a sprinkling of classic vests and romantic, silky shirts with big dramatic sleeves. It was an eye-popping stash, and as I rifled through it, Doug poured himself a big glass of whiskey.

He started telling me the story of his life—how he was raised in an impoverished family and started playing fiddle at the age of five; how his daddy had killed himself when he was seven; how his family moved into a one-room chicken coop after his dad's death; how he started a shoe-shining business when he was eight; and how he began doing drugs at eighteen, eventually becoming an amphetamine addict.

All the while he was telling me these stories, he kept knocking back the whiskey and getting sadder and sadder. I listened intently, incredulous that this musical genius was harboring so much pain. At one point in his storytelling, he was actually crying.

I couldn't believe what I'd gotten myself into, though I was very grateful that he hadn't invited me to his room to come on to me. What he actually needed was someone to talk to.

After about an hour of listening to him, I told him I better be getting home, and he politely accompanied me down to the lobby, where we ran into Joni Mitchell and Ramblin' Jack Elliott.

"Hey, we're all going over to Gordon Lightfoot's house," said Joni. "Wanna come?"

Doug turned to me, but as tempting as the offer was, I just didn't feel confident enough to accept. I was still digesting the unexpected up close and personal encounter with Doug. I figured it was high time to get back to the safety of my parents in the suburbs.

I left Doug then and grabbed the bus home. On the way, I wondered how many other successful musicians were out there on the road, pleasing adoring crowds during performances but quietly crying themselves to sleep at night in hotel rooms. Perhaps that was the price of stardom, of going after your dreams and putting yourself out there. Maybe showbiz wasn't all it was cracked up to be.

Ruminating over Doug's hard-luck story, I realized suddenly how lucky I was to be leading such a privileged life. I had a family who cared for me and protected me. And I was so glad to be on my way home to them.

Dreamy Plaid Lad

Of all the heart-thumping, wildly exciting assignments I've been privileged to get over the years, few rival the opportunity I had in the fall of 1984 to interview Paul McCartney at the Plaza Hotel in New York. Of course, the question of "what to wear" to this monumental life event was of paramount importance. And, it being the opulent eighties, I certainly had a wide array of dazzling garments to choose from. But I went an unexpected route and let more of the warm and honest me shine through by opting for a cozy flannel, black-and-white plaid Roots shirt. I guess I wanted to connect with the unpretentious guy I imagined Paul to be, the guy who lived on a farm in Scotland, light-years away from the pandemonium of that old Beatlemania I'd grown up with.

McCartney had just come out with a lackluster movie called *Give My Regards to Broadstreet,* which needed all the hype it could get. I was lucky enough to have been invited on the press junket to spend a few precious minutes with the pop star I'd idolized for years—and I mean idolized! When I was growing up, Paul's picture hung over my bed, and as a starstruck thirteen-year-old, I thought I'd died and gone to heaven when my friend's grandmother took us to see The Beatles at Toronto's Maple Leaf Gardens. We sat high up in the cheap gray seats and screamed our heads off through the entire show. I can't imagine how I would have felt if I had known that one day, I'd actually have the chance to meet and interview my hero!

I was so nervous on the elevator ride up to the floor where Paul was doing his media interviews. I checked myself in my compact mirror. In my attempt to look as cool possible, I had teamed my Roots shirt with a pair of trendy cream-colored, cotton-twill parachute pants. To give the outfit a little edge, I sported an oversized pair of dangling metal earrings. I was going for the "hip country girl-next door" look, and I think I nailed it. But the butterflies in my stomach were soaring, and I kept hearing my mum uttering one of her favorite warnings: "Just remember: Life is full of disappointments." What if my hero let me down?

I took a deep breath as I walked through the door where the crew was set up. And then I saw him. Paul immediately stood to greet me, something that never happens in junket situations. Our eyes locked, and his face lit up with the most beautiful smile I've ever seen. I immediately felt embraced by his warmth and energy. But what really spoke to me was what he was wearing: a tailored dark green and navy plaid blazer with a black-white-and-red plaid shirt underneath! It was the ultimate in sartorial kismet—we were both wearing plaid!

Paul looked boyishly adorable, and I practically squealed as I greeted him. "Oh hi, I'm Jeanne! I saw you in Toronto years ago!" I gushed, holding myself back from just throwing my arms around him and thanking him profusely for the lifetime of musical magic he'd given me.

"Oh hey, it's you!" he exclaimed. "I remember you—Maple Leaf Gardens—you were up there in the stands!"

He was just winding me up, of course. He most certainly did not remember spotting me high up in the stands. That would have been impossible! But just like that, he'd charmed the hell out of me. No question this guy knew exactly how to work the media. Still, part of me wanted to believe that maybe he did remember seeing me scream my heart out for him back in 1965. Suddenly, I felt like I was thirteen years old all over again.

The connection I felt to Paul was instant, and as nervous as I'd been leading up to this meeting, our conversation felt totally relaxed and natural. We talked about the film, of course, but while I knew I needed to make the most out of the precious few minutes I had with him, I wanted to get as up close and personal with this accomplished icon as I could. I dived right in.

"Do you ever feel obligated to keep trying to prove yourself, whether it be to yourself or to other people?" I asked, trying to understand what drives a supertalent like him to keep on going, to keep on creating.

"Yeah," he said thoughtfully. "I find myself doing that. Sometimes, you get fed up and you think, *Wait a minute, I don't have to prove myself!* So you stop for a couple of weeks or a few days. But then you're doing nothing. And you write a song. You don't write a song to prove anything. You just write it because it's a nice thing to do. You know, it's like a good carpenter is gonna make a table, just because he loves the feel of the wood. I'm the same with music."

I also wanted to understand how this seemingly cool and relaxed guy had come to terms with the incredible pressures of his past, and how liberating it might feel now that the hysteria surrounding The Beatles had waned, at least somewhat.

"Do you ever feel that you've got a lot more freedom now than you had twenty years ago?"

"Yeah, I think so. Because then you've got to listen to what other people want you to do all the time. Now I listen to what other people want me to do only half of the time."

"But don't you ever get nostalgic for that?" I asked.

"I mean, I'm very proud of the old days. And I loved it. I mean most of the time, we had a good time. There were hassles and stuff. . . . But I look back on it with a lot of fondness. And I'm happy about it. And I mean, people like yourself, who can say, 'I was there!' . . . we're all grown up now. We've got kids. I love that. I think it's great."

I was so heartened to hear Paul's wholesome attitude about aging and living in the moment—two things I aspired to in my own life.

I was getting wrapped and just had time for one last question. I figured it should be something all-encompassing, something that would help Paul's legions of fans to really understand his priorities and the lens through which he saw the world.

"What's the greatest lesson that you hope you teach your kids?" I asked.

"Kindness to other people," he offered, without skipping a beat. "I think in our family, we're not really madly academic. Because Linda wasn't a great academic. She was more artistic. And I wasn't very good either. I wasn't very good with the discipline. I had other directions I was wildly interested in, like rock and roll music. . . . Some of the best people I know can't even spell their own name! The point really being that I'm more interested in heart than anything. I think if you've got a decent heart, you'll go a long way."

By the end of our conversation, my own heart was just about exploding. My childhood hero hadn't let me down! To this day, Paul's honesty and utter lack of pretention remain two of the most attractive qualities I've ever encountered in any star I've interviewed. He literally wore his true self on his sleeve, via that simple plaid shirt he had donned that day I interviewed him. The fact that I had unknowingly dressed as his twin was serendipity at its best. It was also a reminder that we're all connected in ways that show on the outside—in fashion—but often go so much deeper than the surface.

A Secret Stash

In 1971 Canadian Prime Minister Pierre Trudeau made headlines when he came under fire for allegedly mouthing a two-word obscenity to his parliamentary colleagues in the House of Commons. When pressed about what he'd mouthed, he asserted it was nothing more than "fuddle duddle."

As a feisty nineteen-year-old, I, like so many other impressionable young women, had quite a crush on the cool PM. He cut a very romantic figure at the time, and his hip way of dressing, whether sporting a dramatic cape or a buckskin jacket, coupled with his shocking irreverence, was the ultimate in cool. I'd never seen a figure who wielded so much political power look so groovy, with a flourish and style all his own.

Handsome and cavalier, Trudeau had a rock star quality

to him. When I discovered a pair of silky orange panties, with a sketch of the Canadian Parliament Buildings and the words "Fuddle Duddle" emblazoned on the crotch on sale at Kresge's, a department store, I bought them immediately. Little did I know that a few months later, those outrageous panties would teach me a lifelong lesson about unconditional love.

But here I am getting ahead of myself. Let's rewind a little. After buying those panties in the spring of '71, I took a summer job at a fine arts camp as a theater counselor. It was the perfect gig for me: I'd been acting professionally since the age of sixteen, and this job would get me out of the city for the summer, working at a place where I could save all my money for my impending move to the Big Apple.

Studying at Montreal's National Theatre School had been my first choice. But the year before, promptly after I'd delivered a monologue from *The Fantasticks* and a soliloquy from *Romeo and Juliet,* the woman behind that school's audition desk had told me, "Well, you're really good. Your energy and stage presence are wonderful, but I think you'd be better performing off Broadway than at Stratford." I'd been a tad crushed. But she wasn't finished talking. "There's a wonderful acting school in New York called the Herbert Berghof Studio, where all the teachers are acting professionals who are simply between gigs. We think that type of school would be great for you."

This made a lot of sense to me, and soon after it was proposed, I began making plans to leave my parents and all the creature comforts that came with home behind and move to New York City.

"So, I'm moving out this fall," I boldly told my parents after dinner one Friday night. There was no doubt in my mind that this was what I wanted, though I was a little apprehensive about how they might react.

"Are you sure you want to go?" my mum asked, the worry already creeping in. "Why would you want to go to New York and live there all alone? You don't know anybody there. Where are you going to live?"

"Ma, I'm sure I'll meet people," I said, showing a confidence I'm not certain I felt. "You know how much I love acting. This is my big dream."

"And Toronto isn't good enough?" she queried.

"Actually, no. Not right now. Not for what I want to do."

There was a deafening silence in the kitchen, and I felt my heart pounding. My father had listened to our back-and-forth without saying a word. How could I ever go without my parents' blessing?

"Okay, *gay gezinta heit!*" he suddenly said in Yiddish. "Go in good health." My beautiful father looked at my mother, and somehow, all the tension ebbed away, because he meant it. He wanted me to pursue my dream.

Hallelujah! Pure joy washed over me as I got up from the table to give both my parents great, big hugs.

In the days leading up to my departure for New York, my mum played the song "Wild World" on our stereo incessantly. It was the year Cat Stevens had come out with his album *Tea for the Tillerman,* and that song—a tune about a young girl going off into the world by herself—was a particular favorite around our house.

As the big day loomed ever closer, Mum put on a brave front, letting Cat Stevens say all the things she couldn't say out loud. One thing she insisted on was to do something her mother had done for her when she left home back in 1937 to go to the big city—Tarnopol, Poland. Apparently, in order to keep my mum's money safe, my grandmother had sewn it into her underpants.

"Mum, that's so creepy. I don't want a stash of cash in my undies," I pleaded when she presented the idea. I was hoping if I protested enough, she'd relent.

"Better safe than sorry," she replied. "It's a wild world out there. You never know what can happen."

Here's the thing: I wasn't even gone yet, and I knew she was already suffering the loss of me, so I decided to indulge my mother with her crazy "safe place" idea. I figured my Fuddle Duddle panties would be the perfect undies for the cause. I handed them over, and my mum neatly sewed a little cotton pocket in the back of them, in which she inserted the $500 I'd saved up from working at camp that summer.

"See how nice this is?" she said when the little hidden pocket was all neatly sewn in. "They'll never find your savings in there," she explained, full of pride and confidence.

And so it was that on my day of departure, I found myself waving from my Greyhound bus to New York City while clutching the fluffy new teddy bear my dad had given me at the bus station and wearing my Fuddle Duddle underwear stashed with cash.

As I waved goodbye, all I could think about was how much my parents must love and believe in me to allow me to go off like that into the wild world, all on my own. As I think about it now, the moment is so raw and memorable. By letting me go, by allowing me to pursue a dream they may not have believed in, my parents taught me the most poignant lesson I've ever learned about selflessness and unconditional love.

Years later, with children of my own now, I understand fully just what a sacrifice my parents made for me that day. Sometimes, to love properly and well, you have to let go of what you love instead of holding it tighter. But as my mother knew, there's always a way to keep someone safe. Sometimes it involves cash and silly Fuddle Duddle panties—a strange gesture of love, but a true one nonetheless.

Itsy-Bitsy Bikini

There's a leopard-trim string bikini nestled at the back of my lingerie drawer that conjures one of the most outrageously playful adventures of my career. In the summer of 2007, I interviewed guitarist extraordinaire Andy Summers of the hot 1980s band the Police.

I first met Andy in 1980, just after the release of the Police's third album, *Zenyatta Mondatta*. The band was touring Western Canada, and as host of *The NewMusic*, I was invited to Regina, Saskatchewan, to do a story on them. I was hugely charmed by all of them, and a few months later, when the band came to Toronto, I was granted a one-on-one interview with Andy.

My cameraman and I visited him in his hotel, where impish Andy encouraged us to push the boundaries of TV propriety.

"I think we should be a little naughty and do the interview from somewhere unexpected," he suggested.

"Okay, we're game!" I said. "What did you have in mind?"

I could see the cogs in his mind turning. And then he lit up. "How about the bathtub?" he proposed.

My cameraman and I cracked up. "Well, I certainly won't be getting in," I said. "But if you're game, sure!"

In the name of rock 'n' roll outrageousness, Andy hopped into the tub wearing a T-shirt but no pants, confident that the wee bottle of hotel-supplied bubble bath he poured into the water would make enough froth to hide his junk. I could hardly contain my laughter as I sat on the edge of the tub, attempting to conduct my serious interview as the bubbles began to dissipate. Andy nervously splashed around, trying to cover himself up to no avail. It was ridiculous and made for great TV—a real music television classic.

Fast-forward to the summer of 2007. More than a quarter of a century after we did our memorable bathtub interview, Andy, who had always had a penchant for photography, released *I'll Be Watching You,* a book of old photos documenting the early, hedonistic days of his life as a rock star. While I was no longer a rock reporter, my producers and I thought it would be cool to interview Andy for *Fashion Television,* since we often covered photography on our show.

My office called to see if he'd be up for a segment. Happily, Andy readily agreed to be interviewed the day after the Police played their concert. He also suggested we do something as outrageous as we'd done all those years ago.

"Maybe this time I'll get into the bathtub with him!" I joked to my producer. My producer mentioned the idea to Andy's management, and they loved it.

So before the big concert, I went backstage and met the band. Sting recognized me immediately and was as gracious and amicable as ever. Andy was happy to see me, too, and we immediately began plotting our shoot for the next day.

"I hear you're thinking of getting into the tub with me," Andy said.

"Well, if I can talk myself into it," I replied nervously, hoping that would be the end of this crazy idea, but the problem with suggesting outrageous ideas is that sometimes people make you follow through with them!

"I've got it all planned," Andy said with a devilish look in his eye. "I'm going to take this rich brocade fabric and decorate the bathroom with it, and I'm going to put candles all around the tub. Rather exotic and mystical, don't you think?"

"I'll bring the bubble bath!" I said, laughing, all while wondering what on earth I'd gotten myself into.

The concert was brilliant. The band sounded as amazing as ever, and I was blown away by their talent, energy, and stage appeal. I was excited for my interview with Andy the next day, and I asked Toronto photographer Paul Alexander to document our interview for *FQ*, the magazine I was editing.

The next morning as I readied myself for the interview, I agonized over whether I should be packing a bathing suit at all—and if so, one-piece or two? After all, I wasn't exactly a young woman anymore. I was a fifty-five-year-old mother of two about to jump in the bath with a rock star!

I told my mother about the plans and the distinct possibility that I would be getting bubbly with Andy.

"You're doing *what*?!" she said. "At your age? Are you crazy?" Mum was appalled I'd even consider such a thing.

I decided to stuff my old string bikini into my purse before I left the house. I figured a one-piece would be too tame if I actually did go through with this crazy plan. "Just in case," I told myself, honestly not thinking I'd really muster the nerve to enter the bathtub.

On my way to the interview, I stopped at the drugstore to buy a big bottle of Mr. Bubble bubble bath. If I was getting in that tub, I wanted as many bubbles covering me as possible!

When I arrived at Andy's hotel suite, he was sitting in the living room picking away at an acoustic guitar. My crew set up a laptop and popped in a DVD of the original 1980 bathtub interview. Andy was transfixed.

But once the video ended, it was time to get down to business. Andy disappeared into the bedroom and emerged a while later wearing a T-shirt emblazoned with the American flag and a drawing of a two-fingered sixties peace sign . . . and (thankfully) a pair of plaid boxer shorts.

"I've just ordered a couple of cosmopolitans from room service," he announced.

Had he ordered drinks because he sensed how nervous I was? I took a deep breath, then headed to the bathroom, where the segment would be shot. True to his promise, Andy had artfully arranged brocade fabric around the tub, along with several lovely candles. The effect was romantic and ultraexotic.

There was no escaping what was next, though. I was almost dizzy with anxiety as I closed the bathroom door and changed into the leopard-trim string bikini I'd stuffed into my purse. As I eyed myself in the mirror, I was determined to fake all the cool and confidence I could muster despite the fact that internally, I was totally freaked out! I wrapped myself in a terry-cloth bathrobe hanging on the door, put my hair up, and emerged from the bathroom. My cameraman, photographer, and even Andy were shocked that I was actually going through with this whole wacky plan!

"Okay, let's do this!" I said with much more confidence than I truly felt.

We were all a little giddy as Andy and I prepared to get into the brocade-trimmed bathtub. Andy turned on the taps, and I reached for my Mr. Bubble bottle, pouring in a generous glug.

Soon enough suds erupted, and Andy, in his baggy briefs and T shirt, gingerly got into the tub. Soaking wet, his clothes were sticking to him in the enormous tub. Suddenly, the diminutive sixty-four-year-old rock star looked to me exactly like a water-logged little boy.

"You coming in?" he asked.

My cameraman started rolling, and summoning every ounce of cool I could muster, I sucked in my gut and disrobed.

As I carefully splooshed into the mass of Mr. Bubbles, arranging myself across from Andy, the cosmos arrived. Andy rested his drink on the side of the tub and then took a joint from the other side and began to light it—not part of the plan, but pure Andy nonetheless!

After a few giggles and repositions, we launched into the interview. Despite the looming lenses and the fact that I was clad in next to nothing, I suddenly felt incredibly at ease. I was actually excited by the thought that I'd be able to share this magical folly with the rest of the world!

I asked Andy what he'd learned about himself from his 1980s rise to fame.

"To be an artist of any kind, you have to operate in a raw, bleeding way," he said between sips of his cocktail and puffs of his joint. "You have to be vulnerable and creative in any sphere. You have to go to a place that's open. . . . It's a balancing act to walk that tightrope of keeping on an even keel yet remaining emotionally vulnerable so you can be creative."

Such sage revelations . . . spoken amidst masses of bath foam!

We were deep in heady conversation about the meaning of art and life when Andy suddenly threw his head back—too close to one of the lit candles. When he leaned forward once more, I screamed in horror: Flames were igniting the top of his head!

I panicked, dropped the mic, and immediately jumped up to douse him. "His hair's on fire!" I yelled.

Two seconds later, before Andy even knew what had happened, the fire was out . . . and invincible Andy just kept on talking! Through it all, my cameraman kept his cool, too, and continued rolling. The resulting footage is some vintage YouTube gold—a video that's been watched by thousands.

By the end of our interview, everyone in that crowded washroom knew what had transpired was magic—an intimate, intelligent, and animated conversation with a bona fide rock star, conducted in a preposterous setting, with a surprise and totally unplanned dramatic twist.

Fortunately, no one was seriously harmed in the bathtub that day. And if I've learned anything from the experience, it's to know when to abandon ego and spontaneously walk on the wild side.

Though I've long since given up wearing bikinis of any sort, that little string bikini occupies a special place in my wardrobe memories. Sometimes it's important to throw caution to the wind. Just be careful no one ignites in the process!

Crowning Glories

Hats have always played a pivotal role in my life, especially during my formative years. First, there was the white straw boater, trimmed with navy grosgrain ribbon, that I got to wear to shul on the High Holidays when I was eight. Then there was the bright yellow, shiny, vinyl rain hat I regularly sported just to get attention in junior high when I was twelve. When I was fourteen, my sister, Marilyn, brought me a fabulous green corduroy Carnaby Street hat from London. I adored the floppy-brimmed, camel-felt number I wore for my first head shot session at the age of sixteen. The red cowboy hat I donned when I traveled back to Toronto after living in New York marked a coming of age for me—I'd survived the Big Apple and was ready to take on the world! And I recall how worldly my chocolate-brown fedora with the pheasant feather made me feel on my first Atlantic crossing on the plane to Paris when I moved there at age twenty-one.

This assortment of *chapeaux* stood for different kinds of empowerment throughout my youth. But for some reason, I abandoned hat wearing in the eighties. Perhaps the mega shoulder pads that ruled fashion during that era were empowering enough. Or perhaps I was with a partner who felt my hats commanded too much attention.

It wasn't until I covered Kate and William's royal wedding in 2011, when fascinators were all the rage, that I dared to don a wee headpiece again. It was a charming turquoise number designed especially for me by Vivien Sheriff, the milliner who designed fascinators for Kate herself.

Being invited to cover the royal wedding was a fantasy of the highest order. Unlike the brutal cost cutting that goes on with most broadcasters these days, the visionaries who were running CTV at the time, Ivan Fecan and Suzanne Boyce, spared no expense when it came to having a Canadian lens on the world.

Besides the handful of newsroom types that got to travel to London for the excitement, there was a team from CTV's popular entertainment show *Etalk,* and me, from *Fashion Television.* To pump up my personal fantasy even more, I was provided with a wardrobe of to-die-for designer pieces to wear on air.

My outfit for the day of the actual wedding consisted of a floral Erdem dress—Erdem Moralıoğlu being a Toronto fashion design student who left Canada for London and has since become a huge success and a favorite of Kate's. I teamed the Erdem dress with a peacock-blue silk jacket from Canadian designer Lida Baday, and a pair of killer aqua and orange patent stilettos by British shoe designer Rupert Sanderson. But the *pièce de résistance* was the feathered turquoise fascinator.

I'd been to England a few weeks prior on a reconnaissance mission, during which I'd visited Vivien at her rural studio near Salisbury, about ninety minutes outside of London. We got along famously, and Vivien offered to design a bespoke fascinator for me.

"The origin of the word *fascinator* is from the male bird's tail feathers, which fascinate his lady friend," Vivien explained. "At this studio, we simply call them headpieces. They're often attached to a little band, or a little comb." Vivien claimed their mass appeal had to do with the fact that they make it easier for onlookers to see one's face, as opposed to the larger hats worn by mothers of the bride.

Needless to say, I was gearing up to feel like quite the fashion queen myself, knowing I'd be reporting from a rooftop across from Westminster Abbey on the morning of the wedding, decked out in my designer finery, a jaunty original creation atop my head, ready for a few hours of live chats with royal fashion experts and sporadic reports about the glorious goings-on around me.

The day before, I had the opportunity to interview a variety of royal style experts, from David and Elizabeth Emanuel, who were responsible for designing Princess Diana's wedding dress, to the late, great Hilary Alexander of London's *Daily Telegraph*. Various luminaries popped by our makeshift set for live hits, and everyone was speculating about who might have received the coveted commission to design Kate's royal wedding gown. Even the bookies had been taking bets for weeks. There was lots of speculation that it might be McQueen, though David Emanuel pointed out that McQueen was owned by Gucci, an Italian company.

"If Kate's gone that route, it would be the first time a British-owned house wasn't chosen," he told me. "And the Italians would have a field day with that."

Personally, I was hoping it might be McQueen. With the celebrated and much-loved designer having taken his life just the year before, and with his extremely capable right-hand woman, Sarah Burton, having taken over the design label, it seemed to me the most fitting choice. But it was all being kept top secret, and Sarah Burton and the house of McQueen were denying any involvement. No one would know for certain who designed Kate's dress until the moment the bride herself stepped out of that big black car. Until then, the world waited with bated breath.

The night before the nuptials, I was talking to my old friend the Canadian-born, London-based designer Todd Lynn. Todd happened to be pals with Sarah Burton, but if she was the one doing the design, she certainly wasn't admitting it.

"I saw something pretty interesting the other night," Todd told me over the phone. "I was passing by the Goring Hotel in Belgravia, where Kate and her family are staying, and I saw someone stepping out of a car with a huge garment bag and going into the hotel with it."

"You're kidding! Is it possible the mysterious wedding dress was in that bag?" I asked. "And do you have any idea *who* was carrying the bag?"

"I couldn't tell. But I did get a glimpse of the shoes. And I could swear they were the kind of little black ballet flats that Sarah Burton always wears!" Todd whispered excitedly. I could tell he was convinced that Kate's wedding gown was a house of McQueen creation, and that cinched it for me. I was pretty sure I had the scoop.

So there I was on the day of the wedding, reporting from my perch. It was minutes before the gorgeous Kate was due to arrive at the abbey. I was feeling both nervous and smug. I knew that I might have the answer to every fashionista's burning question— who is Kate wearing?

Finally, the big moment was upon us. Kate's car was pulled up to the church. I was determined to beat every other reporter to the punch, so a split second before the legendary bride stepped out of that swank 1977 Rolls Royce Phantom VI, I had the chutzpah to tell the world that she'd chosen the house of McQueen to design her gown. It was an educated guess at best, but I just went for it!

As soon as the words were out of my mouth, I heard a collective gasp all around me. And then Kate emerged, resplendent in a magnificent lace and satin gown, which was undeniably McQueen! Tongues started wagging and suddenly "McQueen!" was on everybody's lips. It made perfect sense. Of course it had to be McQueen, since the late designer was so very beloved, so revered, and had risen so meteorically to such iconic heights in his native UK and around the world.

"Congratulations! You were the first to announce it!" my producer offered with a huge smile as soon as our camera stopped rolling.

I felt immense pride that I'd trusted my gut and managed

to scoop everybody else. I also had Todd Lynn to thank for his sleuthing the day before. And I'd be lying if I said I didn't think the soul of McQueen himself was giving me a secret little nudge. I sensed my late pal's spirit that day on that rooftop overlooking Westminster Abbey, head thrown back, roaring with self-satisfaction at all the snooty style watchers covering this historic wedding.

Sadly, Lee was only there with me in spirit, not in reality, and if he'd actually been there, I would have asked him what he thought of my little fascinator. It certainly was a far cry from the dramatic, often outlandish headwear featured in his collections, but somehow, I feel he would have liked me wearing such a whimsical accessory while reporting on such a monumental event on national TV. After all, sometimes it's all about doing what feels right and going with your gut.

Jean Jeanne

When it comes to mainstays in our wardrobes, few would dispute the value of a pair of great-fitting jeans. And in the sixties and seventies, when faded denim was not only the great equalizer among the spirited set but also the hippest style statement a flower child could make, we all owned at least one fabulous pair.

My favorites were Landlubbers, hip-hugging bell-bottoms given to me by a biker named Leif Eriksson, who I met in Miami in 1968 while on Christmas vacation with my parents. Leif was a lanky New Yorker who gave himself that Viking name and smoked an inordinate amount of black hash. I'd gone on a couple of dates with him on his motorbike and had admired his jeans—a brand you couldn't buy in Canada.

The night before I flew back home, Leif generously presented me with his well-worn Landlubber blue jeans. Though ultralong, they fit me well and quickly became part of my uniform, especially for all the times I spent hanging out with my cool pal Debby Solomon.

I first met Debby in junior high, though we didn't get super-chummy until high school. We were both skinny girls with long, dark hair, largish noses, and generous mouths. Not only did we look alike but we also loved the same music, cute boys, fashion, and smoking pot. We had similar glamorous career aspirations, too—Debby wanted to model and I wanted to act. Our birthdays were just one day apart. And we certainly dressed alike—die-hard champions of those bell-bottom, faded jeans, which we regularly rubbed cigarette ashes into to make them look more faded.

I spent countless nights at Debby's parents' house when they were away, staying awake until the sun came up, getting high, and listening to music with my friend. The Moody Blues' "Dawn Is a Feeling" became our anthem, and we'd lie on Debby's living room floor, listening to that fabulous *Days of Future Past* album as we talked about boys and dreamed and schemed about the free-spirited way we were determined to live our lives.

"Jeaaaaaaaaa-nee!" Debby would squeal, always taking delight in stretching my name to the max. "You really are my favorite person in the world," she'd tell me regularly. I couldn't believe it, but I was flattered and savored the thought.

Considering myself a pretty good judge of character, I was constantly counseling Debby on which guys to go for and which to avoid.

"That one's a total creep," I'd tell her, when I knew she was crushing yet again on some shady character. "You're way too nice for him."

"But he's sooooo freaking cute!" she'd lament, as though cuteness could excuse just about everything.

Debby and I shared a spirit of adventure beyond our passion for boys, music, and fashion. As the years passed, our lives took us in different directions. I began to cultivate a media career, while Debby abandoned modeling to train as an interior decorator. When I moved back to Toronto in 1978, Debby helped me furnish my new space. We picked up right where we'd left off, still appreciating each other for that wild teen spirit that burned within us.

The night *The NewMusic*—the trailblazing show that launched my TV media career—premiered in 1979, I watched it with Debby, both of us incredulous that my showbiz dreams were coming true. And over all the years, no matter where we were, we always phoned each other at the stroke of midnight between our two birthdays, just to remind each other of the kindred spirits we were.

Debby's zest for living life large was always inspiring to me, and her warmhearted ways never failed to endear. I introduced her to her first husband, but they eventually split. When I started working at CHUM radio, I introduced her to a cute DJ. They hit it off, and not long after, they got married and had a baby— a beautiful little girl named Joanna, and then another named Veronica. When her husband was offered a big gig in L.A., Debby and her kids followed him there. But I got a heartbreaking call from her once she arrived.

"Well, I moved all our stuff out, and as soon as it all got to the new place, John gave me the bad news."

"Don't tell me he lost his new job!" I said.

"No. The job's going great. But he's leaving me." Debby seemed so matter-of-fact, but I was shocked.

"What? You can't be serious!" I was outraged. I looked around me, at my dear baby girl, who was only a few months old, and my beautiful, cozy home, and my beloved husband. How could I be so lucky when Debby's life had just exploded?

But Debby stayed laser focused, constantly tapping into the idealism and optimism she always had. Eventually, she met someone wonderful, moved to Nashville with him, and had another child. And when that marriage didn't last either, Debby reinvented herself yet again, always hustling and networking to make her way.

The years rolled by, and Debby and I always stayed in touch. She visited me in Toronto, and I went down to Nashville to visit her. Whenever I was in her company, I was transported back to those innocent, dreamy days of our youth, when we were idealistic and carefree and believed anything was possible. And then, somehow, we were turning seventy. On the stroke of midnight, right between our big birthdays, we were on the phone as usual, reminiscing about old times.

"Jeaaaaaaaaaneeee! Can you believe we're *seventy*???? I still feel like I'm seventeen!"

"So do I! Wasn't it just yesterday that we were lying on your living room floor listening to the Moody Blues?"

"Let's try to see each other soon. I really miss you," she said.

"Yeah, me too. Love you, Debby."

"Love you, too. And Happy Birthday to us!"

Exactly two months later, I was diagnosed with breast cancer. Reality was rearing its ugly head: I *was* getting older—physically, anyway. But despite all the fear and uncertainty, I was adamant about staying positive. Somehow, I'd get through this. I started my chemo treatments and prayed a lot. A couple of weeks later, I got a call from Debby.

"Jeaaaaaanneeeee! How are you?"

"Oh, Debby!" I said. "Cancer is no fun, but I am sooooo happy to hear from you!"

"Well, you might not be happy when you hear what I'm about to tell you," she said. I held my breath and waited. "We're in the same club," she added matter-of-factly. "You mean you've got breast cancer, too?" I asked in disbelief.

"Not breast cancer. Stage four lung cancer. And it's spread through my body. But I'm not going down any dark roads, Jeanne. It'll all be okay."

Six weeks later, my dear Debby died. And there I was, still going through weekly chemo treatments, trying to understand how I could be so lucky when my friend's life had ended so quickly. But I knew that Debby wouldn't have wanted me to dwell in the darkness; she was always relentlessly positive. She'd want me to remember our old adventures and lying on her living room floor in our faded blue jeans, dreaming and scheming about life's endless possibilities.

Here Comes the Bride

While garments of all kinds can be rife with memories of special days in our lives, few can compare with the gravitas of wedding ensembles—the gowns, frocks, suits, and accompanying accessories that we don for those sacred, romantic ceremonies and celebrations that stay with us for a lifetime, even if the marriages themselves don't. Having exchanged marital vows twice in my life, I had occasion to dream up two special looks for my big days, each emblematic of a particular era and each a reflection of the disparate ways in which I saw myself as I matured and blossomed.

In keeping with the general zeitgeist, smack dab in the midseventies—1975, to be exact—I couldn't have been more idealistic about life. Having returned from Paris the year before on account of love, my boyfriend, Marty, and I decided to take the leap and get married. He was headed for Newfoundland to continue his studies, so why shouldn't I go along with him as a supportive young wife, and pursue my own evolving dreams? The date for our wedding was set for the eve of our departure, and I was determined to inject as much romance into the occasion as possible. A temple wedding was in order, with a big dinner and dance at the swanky new Sheraton Centre hotel afterwards, complete with a cool jazz band.

As is the case with most brides, the question of what to wear on such a monumental occasion became a major preoccupation for me. Unlike the store-bought, fancy satin and lace concoctions most of my peers were opting for, I was set on creating a bridal statement that was more original. I yearned for something elegant and simple, something that would ooze a romantic kind of modernity. And because I had been wildly inspired by the hooded wedding gown that the gorgeous twenty-two-year-old Margaret Sinclair wore when she wed Pierre Trudeau in 1971, I decided a conventional veil was not the way to go: I would don a hooded jacket over a simple, flowing gown! It would be perfect for the religious ceremony at the temple, where one's shoulders had to be covered. And then I could remove the jacket at the dinner and dance the night away at the reception in the sexy spaghetti-strapped gown. I knew my mum's German dressmaker Mrs. Olson—the same seamstress who had made my Sweet Sixteen dress seven years prior—would do an impeccable job, and I couldn't wait to share my ideas with her.

I went fabric shopping with my mum and came back with a

bolt of a fine white jersey knit, and a couple of yards of gleaming white satin for the lining of the hood and jacket. In the days leading up to the wedding, I paid a visit to a very chic French jewelry store in Toronto's upscale Yorkville called Fabrice and splurged on a small ivory heart to wear around my neck and a matching delicate ivory bangle bracelet.

On my wedding day, I wore my long hair down, adorned with a freesia sprig featuring three white blooms. I never felt more picture perfect in my life. And even though I remember fighting some nagging doubts as I floated down the aisle that afternoon—wondering if perhaps my dad was right when he suggested I was too young to get married, or whether me and my guy were making the right decision by moving to Newfoundland the next day—seeing all those eyes on me, filled with such love and hope, was incredibly heart-swelling. By the time we were at the altar exchanging vows, I gave in to the total romance and idealism of the moment, my confidence buoyed by knowing I was wonderfully dressed for the part.

Fast-forward eleven years: Marriage number one was behind me, although the love for my husband had never really died, and I had spent three of the most amazing years of my life with him in Newfoundland. But, like many couples who join forces at a young age, we simply grew apart. Upon our return to Toronto in 1978, I landed a fantastic on-air job at CHUM radio and a year later, had a dream gig as a Citytv show host. Around that time, my hubby was offered a plum academic job back in Newfoundland, and we both decided to pursue our own career paths. Before long I started making serious money and felt wonderfully empowered, basking in the spotlight of big-city media, knowing I was finally making it on my own terms.

With my biological clock ticking, and having fallen head over heels with the world's cutest CHUM radio DJ—whose on-air name was Bob Magee—I figured it might be time to enter into matrimony once again. Denny O'Neil (his real name) was a wildly romantic and creative soul, and he proposed to me on Christmas Day 1985, through a want ad in the newspaper!

DESPERATELY SEEKING M FACE, it read. (M Face was our cat's nickname and the name of the company I'd started.)

"Let's run away to Switzerland and get married. We won't tell anyone until we're there. Well? Will you marry me?"

It was an irreverent approach to be sure, but endearingly whimsical. I said yes immediately, and our nuptials were slated to take place about six weeks later, on the eve of our Swiss honeymoon departure, at a judge's humble office in Toronto's West End. We realized there'd be too much red tape involved in actually getting married in Switzerland.

Since it was to be the most minimalist affair, with a definite "let's get down to business" vibe, I wanted to wear something smart and stylish, yet powerful and no-nonsense. I had a new royal blue, two-piece gabardine suit in my wardrobe, by American designer Carole Little, that I'd been given by my clothing sponsor to wear on the air. This would be a great way to break it in! The outfit was forties-inspired, with a big-shouldered, fitted jacket and a trim, knee-length pencil skirt. It looked at once professionally polished and a tad romantic. I limited my jewelry to a chunky pair of pearl and crystal clip-on earrings that hugged my lobes and framed my face. And on my feet, a simple pair of black stilettos. I felt as though I meant business in that suit: Now that I had a certain amount of professional success under my belt, I was ready to totally commit to a partner and, hopefully, start a family. But first and foremost, I was a bona fide eighties career woman, and as I sat there, confidently clutching my bouquet, in the back of the limo on my way to the judge's office, I knew I'd finally arrived—no longer merely a dreamer but someone who was actually making her dreams come true.

My marriage to Denny lasted only twelve years, but we produced two gorgeous girls and had untold exhilarating and happy adventures together. And although the end of our marital relationship was filled with pain and sorrow, I was adamant about hanging on to my royal blue wedding ensemble and keeping it safe in my closet, where it remains to this day—a constant reminder of the power and confidence I had when we exchanged our vows—and the inner strength that not only saw me through all the impending sadness but eventually allowed me to rebuild my life. As for my first romantic wedding gown—well, I've lovingly held on to that one as well, a bold souvenir of the old romantic me, who so believed in happy endings. And while I may not have ended up living "happily ever after" with my first husband, that treasured hooded jacket and gown did get a bit of a joyful resurrection recently when my daughter Joey wore it in the music video for her haunting song "Mirroring," all about glimpsing reflections of ourselves that remind us of others. I gather it means she sees bits of me in her, and I can't think of a more profound way for that old wedding gown of mine to not only help make that poignant point but indeed be immortalized.

The Black and White of It

Showing off a baby bump in revealing, skintight garments has become a wonderfully proud and playful thing to do in recent years, but back in the late eighties, pregnant women were a tad more modest about their burgeoning bellies. The context of time is paramount when discussing fashion, and this example proves it.

I have two children, and when I was pregnant, both times, dressing for my new body shape was a challenge. Not only can television make you appear about ten pounds heavier but no one was designing really chic and affordable maternity wear at the time. Designers who were making up-style maternity clothes were creating garments to disguise a woman's pregnancy rather than to feature it. Think oversized smocks and mumus!

The most fabulous dress I ever wore while I was pregnant still hangs at the back of my closet. Though it was never intended to be a maternity dress, it served me and my second pregnancy well. I keep it as a reminder of the insecurities and sensitivities I had at the time, and of my fear that revealing the changes in my body might lead to my being ousted from TV. The dress is made of black crepe and white satin, and features gold-rimmed pearl buttons and a delicate black organza camellia at the neck. Beyond the inherent chicness of this lovely frock, what makes it truly exquisite is who gifted me with it—Karl Lagerfeld.

It was a sweltering July day in Paris in the summer of 1989, and I was seven months pregnant when my cameraman and I headed to the Chanel design atelier for an interview with Karl. It would mark the first time I'd have a one-on-one sit-down conversation with the enigmatic genius, who was famous for his irreverent manner and lightning speed repartee. He'd earned the reputation of being a Renaissance man, boasting a multitude of talents, from clothing design to illustration to his most recent passion, photography, and his larger-than-life personal and style image. And his astounding success at the helm of the revered house of Chanel had won him legions of adoring admirers.

Karl always carried a handheld fan, his trademark, which some believed he held up to his face to cover his double chin. This little detail just added to his list of lovable eccentricities, and I couldn't wait to get up close and personal with him. Still, I was slightly nervous about this encounter with one of fashion's true greats, and sadly, I was feeling bloated and heavy, basically like a beached whale. For the big one-on-one interview, I'd decked myself out in a drab olive-green maternity outfit that was pretty much the antithesis of chic.

When we arrived at the studio, I was on high insecurity alert as I surveyed the room full of gorgeous young women, all impeccably clad in smart, elegant black-and-white ensembles. Everyone was buzzing in anticipation of Karl's arrival.

Because it was the day before the Chanel fall couture collection would be unveiled, the atelier was especially busy, with people scrambling to ready the exquisite garments for their big reveal. I took a seat in the corner of the room, soaking up the action-packed scenario like it was some kind of well-choreographed dance performance. Suddenly, a dashing, impeccably dressed man with heavy rimmed glasses made a beeline for me, arms wide open.

"A pleasure to meet you, Jeanne! I'm Gilles. Sorry, but Karl is running a little late today," he offered apologetically, then quickly added, "And congratulations! When is your baby due?"

"Oh, not until October, but on hot days like this, I really wish it was a lot sooner," I replied.

"Can we get you something to drink? A water perhaps?"

The dapper Gilles Dufour had been Karl's creative assistant for the past six years and was the perfect take-charge host. While he had warned me that Karl was going to be late, as he usually was, I had no idea just how late.

After about two hours of patiently standing by, I was approached by Gilles, who was obviously a little embarrassed by Karl's absence. He came up with a surprising suggestion.

"I'm thinking that maybe you'd like to wear something from Chanel for the interview."

This kind gentleman had noticed my sad olive outfit and was obviously taking pity on me.

While it was a charming suggestion, I balked at first. "Thank you! That is so sweet of you, but I seriously doubt you could find anything I could squeeze into, given the state I'm in," I said.

"Oh, I think we could find something for sure! Why don't you come with me and see?" he said, grabbing my hand.

Gilles escorted me down the hall and into a room filled with racks of sample garments from various Chanel collections. This was the mother lode of *la crème de la crème*—a room replete with a dazzling rainbow of the most sumptuous haute couture pieces imaginable, in the finest silks and satins, punctuated with explosions of organza and tulle. There were elaborate evening gowns featuring eye-popping embroidered details and museum-worthy beadwork, and rows upon rows of delectable tweed and velvet jackets and coats and skirts and trousers, all glittering, some with handmade brocades.

This truly was the height of irony. Here I was being offered the dream chance to try on any one of these fabulous pieces, all in conventional small-sample sizing at a time when my own dress size had ballooned dramatically. I politely perused the racks with Gilles nonetheless, awestruck by this incredible stash of stellar creations.

After a few dizzying minutes, Gilles held something up to me. "What about this one? This could work. It's a loose cut, and it would be very elegant on you."

The dress was black and white, understated, stunning.

"Oh, it's certainly beautiful," I said, "but I'm not so sure . . ."

Gilles insisted I try it on, and just like that, I found myself in a dressing room saying a prayer for the dress to "please, please fit." As proud as I was of my pregnancy, I momentarily wished I was in another body. Off came my drab olive-green ensemble. Wearing just my undergarments, I took a long, hard look at myself in the mirror. I'd never felt fatter or less attractive in my life.

Still, there was this fantasy frock calling out to me from the hanger. I knew I had to at least try it on. I held my breath as I undid the beautiful gold-and-pearl buttons that ran down the front of the dress, then gingerly stepped in and buttoned it up.

I stared at the mirror in joyful disbelief. Voilà! Victory! It fit perfectly! Thanks to the dress's generous boxy cut, and the white satin chevron shape on the front, it had a wonderful slimming effect.

"Guess what?" I playfully called out to Gilles from the dressing room. "It actually fits!" I proudly emerged from the dressing room, striking a little pose as Gilles checked me out.

"*Formidable!*" he enthused. "It really looks great on you."

"Thank you so much, Gilles. Wow! I feel like Cinderella!"

Returning to the studio in a Chanel dress, I suddenly felt much more in tune with the whole chic scenario. Still, we continued to await Karl's arrival.

Another hour later, the master designer made his grand entrance into the atelier, talking a mile a minute and apologizing for his tardiness. He was incredibly excited to show us all the stack of black-and-white photographs he'd just picked up. They were for the next Chanel campaign, shot by Karl himself.

Once the buzzing subsided, we retreated to Karl's office, and as he took his seat behind his big, impressive desk and I sat down across from him, he remarked on how good his dress looked on me.

"*C'est vraiment parfait!*" he said.

I could see from his expression that he was entirely sincere, and this meant the world to me in that moment. "I'm seven months pregnant!" I said. "And still, your clothes make me look wonderful. Have you ever designed maternity clothes?" I asked.

"Yes, once. Only once, for Jerry Hall," he replied.

"You'd be doing a great service for women if you'd consider designing more. There really is a lack of stylish maternity clothes out there."

We launched into our interview and had a very fun and spirited conversation. I thanked him at the end, and again, he said, "I cannot believe how perfect this dress looks on you." He turned to Gilles and said, "*Alors, il faut que ce soit un cadeau pour elle!*"

I couldn't believe my ears—a gift? For me? Karl was actually suggesting that this gorgeous dress would be mine!

"Isn't that wonderful?" Gilles said as he walked me back to the dressing room. "Karl adored you and loved seeing you in the dress. It really is perfect on you."

I changed back into my old outfit and returned the Chanel frock to Gilles, who was standing outside the room with a Chanel shopping bag. He placed the dress into the bag and passed it back to me.

"Thank you so much, Jeanne. We'll see you at the show tomorrow."

The next day, as I took my seat at the Chanel couture show, you can guess what I wore. Clad in my precious haute couture frock, I felt like quite the *grande dame*. I thought about the amazing act of kindness and generosity offered to me by both Gilles and Karl. These men, who really did love women, were obsessed with making them look and feel beautiful. Gilles must have sensed my insecurity from the outset and was determined to make me feel more confident.

The entire experience that day taught me a lesson about the importance of getting over my fears. I was so wrapped up in my insecurities that I almost missed the chance to shine! Sometimes, you have to step out of your comfort zone and just put yourself out there. The worst that can happen is that taking a chance doesn't work. But oh, when it does work—well, the joy is worth the risk.

This singular experience is also a shining example of both the transformational and the empowering nature of clothing. There's no question that wearing that fabulous frock instantly gave me untold confidence—the perfect prep for sitting across from one of the world's greatest designers for an up close and intimate conversation.

Six years later, in December 1995, after I had interviewed Karl many times, we found ourselves about to go on live national TV together. I was the backstage color commentator at the first VH1 Fashion Awards in New York, and Karl and his muse, model Claudia Schiffer, were standing by for an interview. We were about a minute to air when Karl suddenly panicked, realizing he'd misplaced his handheld fan. It was unthinkable that he'd appear on national TV without his signature accessory.

"*Merde!*" he snapped, just about ready to walk out of our shot.

My instincts kicked in. I looked around and saw some sheets of cardboard resting on a table nearby. "*Une seconde!*" I said, as I grabbed a sheet and gingerly began folding it back and forth, accordion style.

A few seconds later, I held up my makeshift cardboard fan. "*Voilà!*" I said. "*Pour toi.*"

Karl was utterly delighted as I presented him with the paper fan.

Suddenly, the director was counting down to airtime, and then I was firing questions at Karl, which he answered beautifully, all while working his cardboard prop with his usual aplomb.

Two minutes later, our interview was complete, and the camera was off us.

"*Ah, c'était parfait, non?*" he said to his PR person, who was standing by. He turned to me then and said, "I always love your enthusiasm!"

The next thing I knew, he was reaching forward and wrapping me up in a warm hug.

Isn't it interesting how we're all the same? All of us, even the biggest style icons in the world, have moments of insecurity. Isn't it just a matter of kindness to help others regain their sense of self when, for whatever reason, they lose it?

We're only human, after all.

Dressing the Part

Imagine a pair of skintight black vinyl jeans. What do they make you think about? What would such a garment mean to you?

Back in the day, that supercool garment became my wardrobe go-to piece for interviewing rock stars. While faux-leather leggings have become trendy in recent years, in the eighties, wearing black vinyl anything was extremely cutting edge. I loved my black vinyl jeans because I could dress them up or down, and they oozed edginess and always made me feel sexy.

Those were the jeans I wore to a concert in the summer of 1981, when an open field in Oakville, Ontario, became a rock music playground for some 25,000 fans. The event was dubbed the Police Picnic, with British pop band the Police headlining, and there was an impressive roster of punk and New Wave bands on the bill, including legendary rocker Iggy Pop, a native of Detroit, who was the epitome of cool.

I knew that Iggy wasn't the easiest guy to interview. He could be a little tough and irreverent. But the last time I'd interviewed him, he'd been pretty civil to me. So, I was assigned the task of buttering Iggy up once again for our Police Picnic coverage, hoping he'd make nice with our camera. I was on my guard, but I was determined to charm the notorious punk rocker.

My producer had accompanied Iggy into the field just a short distance from the trailers where the musicians were lounging. Dressed in my vinyl jeans and a short-sleeved black sweatshirt with open gold zippers running along the shoulders, I was feeling cool and confident as my cameraman and I approached our shooting location. Iggy was knocking back a bottle of Jack Daniel's when I walked up to him, and the minute my cameraman started rolling, Iggy cozied up to me and was extremely affable.

"Hi! It's nice to see you again," he said.

"Nice to see you, too," I replied, relieved he was in a good mood.

We talked about his recent European tour, and he sang the praises of Portuguese food. Then suddenly, he changed the subject. "Do you know, I was trying to pick you up earlier on?"

I couldn't believe what I was hearing. Nothing that had transpired had suggested that intent, but here was Iggy Pop flirting with me on camera and giving me some really great sound bites! "If only I would have known!" I said with a little laugh.

"I kept saying to my people, 'Who's that chick?'" said Iggy, now eyeing my vinyl jeans.

While in this day and age, Iggy's lascivious behavior would not likely be tolerated, sadly, it was par for the course in my industry four decades ago. I played nice, all while thinking about what I could say to take Iggy's mind off my pants. I started asking more questions about his performance plans and upcoming tours. He was his usual irreverent self, but he answered my questions, and my jeans and I got through the entire interview with all the footage I needed.

Fast-forward to four months later at my parents' house in the suburbs after a relaxed, late Friday night dinner. It was around 11:00 when the phone rang. It was my *NewMusic* show producer, John Martin.

"We need you down at the Danforth Music Hall," he told me. "How quickly can you make it there?"

"What do you mean?" I asked. "Tonight?"

"Yes, tonight. We just got you an interview with Iggy as soon as he gets offstage!" John replied.

I wasn't thrilled to make the midnight trek down to the concert hall, especially after not having seen the show. And I certainly wasn't dressed for the part. After all, I was at my parents' place for a Sabbath dinner, clad in a conservative red sweater and a pair of suede khaki trousers. With my big fox overcoat on top of it all, I looked like the furthest thing from a rock chick, but duty called, so I scrambled into my little VW Beetle and made the thirty-minute drive downtown.

By the time I got there, the fans had all departed, but the doors were still open, and I made my way to the basement dressing room. I looked through the open door, and there was Iggy, slouched in the corner with one of his bandmates, both of them drinking whiskey out of paper cups. There was a handful of other guys in the crowded room, all clad in old jeans and funky T's, ultracasual, ultracool, and high on the show Iggy had just given.

I took a deep breath and swooshed in, feeling a little too conspicuous in my ostentatious fur. Quickly removing my coat, I tossed it on a chair and moseyed up to Iggy, who by the sound of his laughter, was totally relaxed.

"Hey, hi, Iggy!" I said, warmly.

"Hey," he said, looking me up and down. I thought for sure that after our last encounter, he'd remember me, but he didn't. Suddenly, there was an edge to him that I hadn't felt before.

I settled into a chair across from him, and taking my cue from my cameraman, I casually launched into the interview, talking about his newly recruited musicians and then touching on a book he was writing about his first band, The Stooges.

"So, is this your first attempt at writing?" I asked.

Iggy stared at me with a smirk on his face. "Attempt?" he fired back, clearly insulted.

The conversation continued, but I knew I'd messed up. I tried a few other angles, but I didn't get very far with any of them. Iggy was growing nastier and more ego-inflated by the minute.

"It's easier for me to achieve because I have more talent in any area than you could ever dream of," he said.

"How the fuck do you know that?" I shot back coolly.

"Someone with your own limitations should stick to what they do very carefully," he hissed.

I was blindsided, but I looked Iggy right in the eye. "You really are something else," I said.

"In other words, you're about to say I'm a cunt, but you're more of a cunt than I am. You just hide it," he replied.

I was flabbergasted, not just by his language but by the disrespect. "Okay, that's a wrap," I said. For the first time in my career, I walked out of the interview before it was done.

Standing up and grabbing my fur coat, I gave him one last look. "Gee, Iggy," I said, not knowing what else to say.

"I'm happy to talk to you," he insisted. "I'm not insulting you. I'm honoring you."

"You're honoring me?" I replied. "I don't think so . . ."

"Anything else I can do to convince you?" he pleaded.

I refused to answer.

"Well, I'm sure you can do a good cut-up job," he said. Evidently, it had suddenly occurred to him to be concerned about what he'd just said.

"No," I replied. "I wouldn't waste my time. Bye-bye."

With that, I left the room.

Watching the video of that awkward backstage adventure—which has had thousands of views on YouTube—I'm proud of myself for standing up to that man, especially at an early stage of my career.

I do still ask myself just why Iggy turned on me when our previous interview had gone so well. Was he posturing in front of his male buddies? Was it something I said? Or was it something I wore?

Sometimes, clothing can provide a kind of armor—protection

of sorts—and sometimes it does exactly the opposite. To this day, I wonder if my boring red sweater and conservative pants set the punk rocker off. Was I, in his eyes, just some bourgeois uptown gal who had no clue about the gritty struggles of a *grand artiste* like him?

I'll never know for sure what went so awry that night, but the whole episode made me more sensitive to how quickly men in my industry perceived women's manner of dress . . . and judged us for it. I wonder how differently things might have turned out if I'd been wearing those tight vinyl jeans I'd worn last time.

That one encounter taught me how important it is not to take abuse from anyone, ever. And for that reason, if not for any other, I suppose that interview was a huge success.

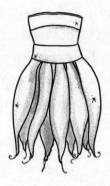

Style Is About Attitude

So many wardrobe pieces that we hold on to over the years remind us of special people who have played pivotal roles in our lives. And while we may never even think of resurrecting some of these pieces, we hold on to them as vestiges of times in our lives—and reminders of the amazing people who helped inspire us. Case in point: For over four decades, I've kept a designer gown not because I thought I'd wear it again but because of the person who gave it to me.

The gown in question was designed by Wayne Clark—a white satin number with an organza petal skirt studded with rhinestones. It was a gift to me from the late Canadian artist and legendary Olympic skating star Toller Cranston. He presented it to me not long after we met, and it was unquestionably the most glamorous and extravagant gift I'd ever received.

Toller came into my life rather serendipitously. A big fan of the show Ice Capades when I was growing up, I'd always adored the unabashed glamour of sequined skaters. But I never imagined what creative heights the sport would scale until Toller Cranston wowed the world at the 1976 Olympics. Glued to my TV screen for his Olympic performances, I was fascinated by how he changed the entire sport of figure skating seemingly overnight.

He'd scored a bronze medal at those Olympics—something that was always the bane of his existence, since he felt he deserved gold. And so did I. Here was an athlete who wasn't about tricks and jumps; rather, he brought drama, grace, and sheer theatrics to the ice. To me—and to countless other Canadians—he was such an inspiration. And because I'd been studying mime in Paris just a couple of years earlier and was totally mesmerized by the art of corporal expression, I considered Toller a true, trailblazing creative genius and quite simply, my artistic hero. I hung a newspaper clipping of him wearing a large black hat over my desk at the CBC radio building, where I worked from 1975 to 1978. And that was before I'd even met the man!

In the summer of '78, I moved back to Toronto, and a year later, I found myself working for Citytv, cohosting the groundbreaking music magazine show *The NewMusic*. Unbeknownst to me, Toller was a big fan of our show. Through a friend, I heard that his skating coach was renting out a small attic apartment across the street from Toller's house in Toronto's Cabbagetown neighborhood. My friend introduced me to Toller's coach, and before I even knew what was happening, I found myself in Toller's sunny kitchen, being offered a coffee and grilled by the legendary skater himself.

On a break from his studio, Toller was at his casual best, wearing paint-splattered chinos and an oversized paint-splattered white shirt. I was fascinated by his paint-stained fingernails, which he regularly dragged through his unruly hair like some mad composer. How different he looked from that pristine performer and impeccable showman I'd been so inspired by, clad in all those dazzling costumes!

"Oh, you're the one on that music show," he commented with a kind of cool curiosity. "I can't understand how you can talk to those spaced-out rock stars!" Evidently, Toller had just seen the interview I'd done with the legendary punk musicians the Ramones. One of them, Johnny Ramone, kept staring into the camera on the wide shot, looking totally detached. Even I don't know how I managed to keep the conversation going with the other guys in the group when that one member seemed so spaced out.

"Yeah, that's me," I said with a laugh. "I guess you've just got to stand your ground and not take any of it too seriously."

Toller immediately started asking me about some of the enigmatic characters I'd met, and suddenly, I felt like the one who was being interviewed—a rarity in my business.

It was thrilling for me to see this other side of Toller, and by the end of our coffee meeting, he decided that I must rent his coach's attic apartment. "It'll be great fun," he promised. "Besides, I'm ordering you to move in!" he said with a laugh, letting me know who was boss.

Toller and I became fast buddies, and he took great delight in regularly grilling me about my love life and always offering outrageous counsel, like telling me the kind of man I should consider pursuing, or suggesting the types of provocative outfits I should be wearing to attract the right guy. He became my closest confidant, and most interestingly, he became my style adviser, too. He believed I should put every penny I made on my back.

"What else do you really need to spend your money on?" he asked. "Nothing is more important for you at this stage of your career—and your life—than image. It'll be what makes or breaks you in the business," he told me. "Clothes are how everyone judges you."

If there was anyone who understood the impact clothes could make, it was Toller. And while I didn't entirely agree with the idea of spending all my money on clothes, I did learn a lot from him.

Every day I'd watch from my window as he took his two English setters, Lapis and Minkus, for walks. He would always be decked out in dramatic hats and colorful cashmere sweaters, oversized overcoats and capes, and ultralong scarves. To me, his extraordinary sense of style wasn't just about *what* he was wearing—it was *how* he chose to wear his clothes and the manner in which he moved. That, I decided, was what true style was all about.

Nonetheless, when he asked me to be his date for the 1981 Genie Awards, I immediately started to fret. "Seriously? You want me to go to the Genies with you? And be on the red carpet? What on earth am I going to wear?" Being on the arm of a showman like Toller called for something extraordinarily special.

"Oh, we'll figure out something," he replied cavalierly. These were the days before *Fashion Television,* and the only local designers I had access to were rock 'n' roll ones. But they were too fringe for a film academy's red carpet.

Toller, however, had a solution. He showed up at my door one night carrying a huge box with a big red ribbon around it. "I saw this in the window and knew it was you!" he said, smiling widely.

We went inside, and I excitedly opened the box. Under all the tissue was the most jaw-dropping white gown I'd ever seen. It was like something out of *Swan Lake*—unlike anything I'd ever owned. It looked like a dress a fairy queen would wear. With its strapless white satin bodice, it had a skirt made of countless huge white organza petals. Long thread tendrils dripped from the tips of the petals, many of which were studded with tiny sparkling crystals. This was a fantasy frock of the highest order.

"Are you *serious*? This is for me?"

"Yes! It's a Wayne Clark. I was walking past a shop window when I saw it and immediately thought it screamed you. Go try it on!" Toller insisted.

I scooped up the lavish creation and disappeared into the bedroom, incredulous that this gorgeous garment was being given to me. It fit like a glove and looked amazing.

Toller could not have been more pleased with himself for making the choice. "Perrrrrrfect, my love," he swooned. "It was definitely made for you! Jaws will drop, I know...."

When Toller and I stepped out of the limo and onto the red carpet for the Genies a couple of weeks later, we were one of his fantasy paintings come to life. At the fancy gala, I instantly stood out from the crowd.

Toller was delighted with the image of us that night. He'd done such a brilliant job styling me, and though we were most certainly not a couple in the usual sense, he exuded a special pride with me on his arm that night. The whole evening felt like a coming-out party for me: My TV career was taking off; I had a bona fide celebrated luminary as my closest confidant; and now, I had the right designer fare to strut. "*CityTV*'s Jeanne Beker projected a refined razzle-dazzle in a rhinestone-dotted white organdy gown by Wayne Clarke," the *Globe and Mail* reported the next day. I felt as though I'd arrived.

I've often thought that choosing that frock was Toller's way of costuming me for the role he saw me playing in his life—someone through whom he could live vicariously. He used to quiz me about the details of my dating life, always analyzing the politics of my love relationships—past, present, and future. In the weeks leading up to the gala awards and in the subsequent months and even years, Toller would always refer to that Wayne Clark creation as "The Dress"—as though this garment was the epitome of all dresses, a revered third party in our friendship.

While I only wore "The Dress" one more time before retiring it, I most certainly wore other Toller concoctions regularly. One of the wonderful things about him was his incorrigible naughty streak. He loved to egg me on, to challenge me to do and say things he wouldn't normally dare to.

There was one time he urged—practically ordered—me to wear a sexy black corset, panties, and fishnet stockings (and nothing more) to an elaborate dinner party he was hosting at his home, dubbed the Banquet in Black.

"You must!" he insisted. "That getup will be *le dernier cri*! You can totally get away with it. Just think of how empowered you'll feel when no one will be able to take their eyes off you!" And with that, he let out one of his signature howls of laughter, delighted by the outrageous scenario he was concocting in his mind's eye.

I'd just covered a downtown gallery exhibit devoted to Madame X, an American expat who married a French banker and became notorious in Parisian high society circa 1889 for her beauty and rumored infidelities. The exhibition featured a host of kinky corsets and other sexy accoutrements worthy of a brothel. I found Madame both amusing and inspiring, so I knew exactly what to draw on for my Banquet in Black getup.

While I didn't go quite as far as Toller wanted me to with my outfit, I did buy a little riding crop, which was a tad daring, to be sure—the ultimate accessory.

Toller's eyes lit up when I showed it to him. "Perfect!" he roared. "Now you'll just have to practice working it."

At the dinner, Toller mischievously sat me next to Ivan Fecan, the dashing head of CBC TV at the time. I'd worked for him briefly when he was the news director at Citytv. If anything could further my career, this close encounter could . . . or so thought Toller.

Though I might have made a memorable impression on Ivan that night, somehow I didn't suddenly make it to mainstream prime time the way Toller was convinced I would. Still, after I got over my initial shyness at that dinner, I had a grand time. I also had no regrets about my outrageously daring costume, though it may have hurt my credibility with our national broadcasting network.

In January 2015, I got a shocking call out of the blue. Toller, my friend, my mentor, had been found dead in the garden at his villa compound in San Miguel, Mexico. Apparently he'd suffered a heart attack in the middle of the night. I was gutted, especially to think that he'd died all alone.

To this day, I think of Toller all the time. He remains the most colorful person I've ever known. Deep in my closet, "The Dress," that gorgeous white flight of fancy, still hangs proudly as a testament to the man who taught me the importance of flash and flamboyance. But style always went far beyond clothes with Toller. Clothing was merely window dressing. It was attitude he promoted most of all, and that's a lesson he taught me that I'll never forget.

Dazzled by Dior

The very first year *Fashion Television* was on the air—1985—my crew and I were invited to Paris to do a story on Christian Dior. That year the illustrious house had been purchased by French entrepreneur Bernard Arnault, and evidently he was eager to get as much exposure for the legendary label as possible.

My crew and I were flown to Paris first class and put up at the luxurious Bristol Hotel. Visiting the chic Dior boutique on Avenue Montaigne for the first time was a total fantasy. Beneath the opulent crystal chandeliers, everything was bright and beautifully buzzing, with a sale going on. Dozens of well-heeled women emblazoned with Dior accessories were picking through the tables laden with lacy lingerie, all looking for a bargain even though money was no object to them. I watched and I yearned to look like them, talk like them, smell like them, and shop like them.

Thankfully, I didn't stand out too dreadfully because the Dior PR woman had loaned me a lush burgundy cape to wear for my meeting with the label's designers—Marc Bohan, who did the ready-to-wear, and Frédéric Castet, who designed all the furs and leathers.

I floated up the long, plush staircase to visit the design studios and meet the two men who were creating the Dior fantasies. Castet, who'd worked at the house since the days of Christian Dior himself, was a short, charming, silver-haired gentleman in a black leather jacket. His creations were totally drool-worthy, with some in the $100,000 range. Castet certainly kept the Dior atelier inspired and busy, with imaginative lavish beading and exquisite embroidered details on so many of the items. His specialty was working with exotic furs and rich, supple leathers, and these materials would be dyed in the most sensational colors. I recall one eye-popping coat made of fur and leather in a rich rainbow of colors, pieced together to look like a stained-glass window.

In the early days of *Fashion Television,* because it was a show of "reporter involvement," I often modeled designers' pieces for our camera. We figured it would be fun for the folks at home to see a "real woman" in some of these outrageous high-end clothes. And Castet's over-the-top creations provided the perfect theatrical fare for my modeling antics.

The *pièce de résistance* in that collection was a faux-jewel-encrusted, black-leather-and-suede dress with mega shoulder pads and a sizable plastic peekaboo hoop at the hip. The whole creation was kinky, revealing, and totally original—a true eighties fashion statement.

Castet saw me admiring the brash and bold dress and said, "It's you. It's totally you."

I discreetly checked the price tag—about 40,000 francs, or $8,000—way out of my league! But Castet insisted I try it on. Happily, it fit perfectly! I came out of the dressing room feeling like the ultimate Dior diva.

"*C'est fabuleux!*" said the designer. "It looks so good on you!"

"I feel amazing in it. How lucky that I can wear it for our interview."

The camera started rolling, and we launched into our delightful conversation just outside the dressing room.

When the interview was over, I took the dress off and put it on the showroom rack. I left Dior with an "Oh well, maybe next lifetime" feeling—grateful that at least I'd had the chance to actually strut the fabulous creation for a few fleeting minutes.

On the way back from Avenue Montaigne, my producer and I were in a fashion-hungry, devil-may-care mood, so we dropped into the big Galeries Lafayette department store and made a beeline for the crowded hat department. In the name of fun, I tried on a few swish *chapeaux,* playfully modeling them in front of the busy mirrors, drunk with happiness over the transformational possibilities of fabulous French fashion.

Suddenly, I looked down at my purse. *Mon dieu*—it was wide open! My heart sank as I pulled the purple fedora off my head and quickly looked inside. My worst fears were confirmed: My wallet was gone! I'd been pickpocketed. I panicked as I thought about all the credit cards and cold hard cash I'd stashed in that bag. What an idiot I was! How could I have been so careless? There went eight hundred dollars and all of my ID!

I dashed off to find customer service, even though I knew I'd likely never see my wallet and its contents again. The woman at the counter suggested I make a report to the police, but other than that, she said, "There's not much we can do. *C'est la vie.*"

Suddenly, I hated everything French and went back to my hotel frustrated and totally deflated. That night my crew and I dined with one of the Dior PR women. I told her about my discouraging experience.

"Oh, I'm so sorry," she said. "That's really unfortunate. But I hope it won't turn you off returning to the boutique tomorrow to interview the other designers. We were really hoping you'd come back."

I assured the Dior rep that of course I would be there. After all, even if I didn't feel like going anywhere ever again, I still had a job to do.

I went back to Avenue Montaigne the next morning, eager to get my interviews over with so I could leave corrupt French society forever. My conversation with Marc Bohan went well. The PR people thanked me and the crew afterwards, and just as I was about to leave the store, one of the PR women came out of a back room carrying a big shiny box tied up with ribbon.

"This is a *cadeau* for you," she said sweetly.

I was completely confused. "For me?" I said. "Really?"

She nodded and waited as I excitedly opened the box. Inside, sitting on a bed of tissue, was an envelope, addressed *Mlle. Beker.*

I opened it and inside was a card that read: *Tu es vraiment merveilleuse dans cette robe.* You look truly marvelous in this dress. *Merci mille fois! Tu es charmante.* A thousand thank-yous. You are charming.

It was signed *Frédéric Castet.*

I couldn't believe it. I peeled away the layers of tissue to find the leather-and-suede, jewel-encrusted dress I'd tried on the day before! I was overwhelmed with emotion.

"This is incredible!" I gushed. "I don't know what to say. Thank you so, so much. This is the most amazing gift! So generous of you. *Merci mille fois!*"

Absurd as it sounds, in that moment the French redeemed themselves. I kicked myself for having been so dark and petty and vindictive about an entire culture. How could I have doubted a whole society based on one bad experience? How could I have lost faith in everybody just because one crook had wronged me? Bad things happen to everybody everywhere. But it's also true that when you least expect it, acts of kindness, like tiny miracles, illuminate life anew.

That gorgeous black Dior dress is one that I cherish to this day. Although I haven't worn it since the eighties, it serves as a valuable reminder that sometimes magic can happen just when you're about to give up.

Party Dress

Planning my Sweet Sixteen party was one of the most exhilarating things ever. And when you're a teenage girl, nothing beats sharing an exciting experience with a bestie. Marsha Rocket was that to me—a brainy and beautiful gal who lived around the corner and who always exuded strength and savvy. She not only turned me on to smoking Kool menthol cigarettes and introduced me to off-white lipstick and shiny black eyeliner but also encouraged me to conscript Brian Ceresne, the cutest boy at our high school, to be my date and the "host" of my Sweet Sixteen.

Of course, when it came to the most vital question, what to wear to the big event, we pored over my mum's fashion glossies and decided that the skintight, sparkling turquoise blue minidress with matching boots featured on the cover of the December 1967 issue of *Harper's Bazaar* would be the perfect choice. There was just one problem: Purchasing such designer fare was totally out of the question.

And that is why I enlisted my mother, who took me to Stitsky's, the giant fabric store in downtown Toronto. There we found just the right material to give my mum's German dressmaker so she could knock off the delicious designer outfit.

Much to my chagrin, I never realized that the dress on that magazine cover was a stretchy knit. The sparkly fabric I bought had no give to it at all, so to get the skintight look I was after, the dressmaker had to sew zippers along the forearms. And the "boots"—which were actually stockings—also had to be tight-fitting, so the dressmaker concocted zippered footwear for me as well. Now I just had to find a pair of turquoise shoes large enough to stuff my fabric-wrapped feet into!

Marsha came to the rescue and accompanied me downtown on the hunt, and we miraculously found—on sale—the perfect pair of oversized turquoise patent heels. When I put it all together—the wild skintight dress and the turquoise heels—it was the most sensational outfit I'd ever owned. I'll never forget that knowing look in Marsha's eyes as she nodded at me across the dance floor the night of my party, signaling that I'd done well. I felt empowered, knowing that fashion-savvy Marsha approved.

That summer Marsha persuaded me to attend an open audition she'd read about in the paper. The CBC was casting a new sitcom about the trials and tribulations of being a teenage girl, and my bestie knew I had the burning desire to be an actress. I had no acting experience whatsoever, but with Marsha's relentless cajoling, I not only got up the nerve to audition for a part but eventually landed it!

I didn't get the good news right away though, and I was dismayed after not hearing back after a couple of weeks. Marsha decided that what I needed to lift my spirits was a bit of an image change. She convinced me to go for a hip new look by lopping off my waist-length hair and replacing it with a trendy pixie cut—the style that Mia Farrow had started sporting as the character Allison on the hot TV series *Peyton Place*. Marsha held my hand at Toronto's legendary Gus Caruso Salon as I entered a new age and gained a new sense of self in the process.

As the years went by, I lost touch with Marsha, though I know she followed my career closely. On occasion, since she'd become a popular wedding planner, I'd run into her at a wedding, and she'd always tell me how impressed and proud she was of what I'd accomplished.

One day in the fall of 2021, we decided to have a reunion of a handful of high school besties, and I had the joy of sitting next to Marsha at a restaurant, reminiscing like crazy, both of us incredulous that we were turning seventy the following year.

"Promise me we won't lose touch again," I said.

"Oh, you got it," said Marsha.

I knew she'd been going through a very stressful time. Her husband was in dire need of a kidney transplant, and her eldest daughter had proved to be a match. Marsha was understandably nervous about the surgeries to come. We texted each other on the day of the transplant operation about three months later. I was amazed that my old friend seemed so strong and calm. Thankfully, all went well.

But that spring, ten days after my seventieth birthday, I received some devastating news: Marsha had died. She'd complained of back pain the night before, and on her way to the doctor's the next morning, in the car, her heart gave out. She was gone, just like that.

It was unthinkable that this human firecracker could be extinguished so abruptly. Once the initial shock wore off, I mourned for all the years I could have had Marsha in my life but didn't. I went to the shivah and met Marsha's five beautiful daughters for the very first time. I was down on myself for not having made a concerted effort to have Marsha be a part of my life for all those years. But this tragic experience got me thinking about what a profound influence my old friend had been on me, and how I really did carry her in my heart constantly, even though I went years without seeing her.

Marsha's encouragement in those early years of our friendship undoubtedly ignited passions in me to pursue my aspirations; she always seemed to think anything was possible, and her faith was so strong it rubbed off. Bringing a fashion fantasy to life? No problem. A career in television? Absolutely!

I didn't know it at the time, but that sparkly Sweet Sixteen ensemble proved to be a harbinger of things to come for me, showing me that high-fashion dreams and glamour were indeed within reach. Marsha had a vision of what I was destined for long before I did, and I'm grateful to her to this day for seeing what I couldn't. Sometimes a good friend and a good outfit are all you need to see you through.

Red-Hot Booties

Though you might expect that my wardrobe is jam-packed with luxury designer labels, I've rarely purchased that kind of costly fare. There have been a precious few times over the years that I've actually gone out and splurged on designer items, but I've been fortunate enough to have been gifted several amazing things.

One memorable splurge occurred in early 2010, when I found the most wonderful bright red Alexander McQueen high-heel booties on sale at one of my favorite New York shoe emporiums. I simply couldn't resist forking out my hard-earned dough for them. I'd never owned anything by Alexander McQueen before, which made my flashy find all the more precious. These boots made such a strong statement. I wasn't sure where I'd actually wear them, but just to own something that sported the coveted McQueen label was satisfaction in itself.

A few weeks after my big purchase, I got the plum assignment of covering style at the Vancouver Winter Olympics. When it came to planning my on-air looks, I knew my fresh red footwear would provide the perfect punctuation to at least one of my stylish outfits, so I happily packed them in my bag. I could never have imagined that on the second day of the Olympics, I'd get a heartbreaking call from my producer telling me that McQueen had taken his life. I was in tears as I donned my precious McQueen boots, preparing to record my *Fashion Television* stand-up about the devastating news.

From the moment we first met, I felt a strong connection to the brilliant and bold designer. Lee McQueen's irreverent humor, naughty nature, and unbridled laughter endeared him to me immediately. But I also saw the other side of McQueen— the pained, misunderstood, sensitive artist whose love of design, craftsmanship, and storytelling knew no bounds. McQueen was a poet at heart and never failed to charm me with his passion and honesty. We'd had some spirited and revealing conversations over the years. I knew he appreciated my enthusiasm, and I felt as though we were kindred spirits.

I first had the chance to spend some real quality time with McQueen in 1995, when we were on the judging panel of the Smirnoff International Fashion Awards in Cape Town. I was married at the time, and McQueen briefly met my husband. But three years later, after my husband left me, McQueen was so sympathetic when he found out. Every time we saw each other after that for an interview, he'd ask, "How's your love life?" I tried to keep him up to date as best I could, and I think he really appreciated our personal exchanges. Our human connection was simple but elegant. It went far beyond mere fashion chat.

When I attended a McQueen spring show in 2000, I was delighted to catch up with him backstage.

"Guess what?" he said, just as my cameraman was preparing to roll. "I got married! Meet my husband, George." He then introduced me to a mild-mannered, dapper guy sitting a few feet away. "Haven't said anything publicly yet, but we got married a few weeks ago on a yacht in Ibiza."

"How fantastic!" I said, excited to think that my designer friend was trusting me with a bit of a scoop. "I'm so, so happy for you."

Over the years McQueen and I deepened our connection, one interview at a time. As entertaining and engaging as he was, he was also very thoughtful and philosophical. He frequently pointed out that everything in life was a lesson. When he made his New York debut, in 1996, he kept key fashion editors waiting to get into his show and then actually locked some of them out on purpose. We had a good laugh over that the following day.

I remember his pain when he took over the legendary house of Givenchy and how the critics mercilessly criticized his work. "I was twenty-six when I went to Paris," he reflected when I interviewed him in 2006, five years after he left Givenchy. "I'd only been out of college for two years and was the head of a French couture house. I was thrown to the lions, and the only person feeling it was me."

At another time McQueen told me, "Fashion is a big bubble and sometimes I feel like popping it."

Like the rest of us who've worked in fashion's trenches, he knew that the business was about selling fantasies, and he recognized that he was a master purveyor of illusion with his unbridled creativity and heady storytelling. But despite his preoccupation with fantasy fare, I always felt McQueen was after truth, in both his work and his life.

When I interviewed him in the summer of 2006 in San Francisco, just before he received an honorary doctorate from the Academy of Art University, the Dalai Lama's book *The Art of Happiness* was on his hotel room coffee table. I remember looking from him to the book and feeling so pleased that he had found some grounding and strength.

"There comes a time in life when you don't have to spell out for so many people what you're about," he told me that day. "I was so determined to drum into people what I was like that I forgot what I was actually doing, which is fashion. And it became so much about a show. But now it's a balance," he shared. "And as well as a show, the collection itself is poetic."

I asked him if he felt that the fashion business was a lonely one. He thought long and hard before answering.

"It can be. And I think there's more to life than fashion. . . . You see, everyone else in the office, they can go home and chill out. But I'm still Alexander McQueen till I shut the door. I've got to go home with myself. And if I've had a bad day, I've only got myself to answer to."

McQueen's masterful designs continued to wow us those

next few years as he worked through his continuing loneliness. He shunned requests for TV interviews, though I did manage to briefly catch up with him backstage just before he sent his final, Atlantis-inspired collection down the runway in October 2009. I was doing my usual backstage running around when I noticed McQueen sneaking out the door for a smoke. Leaving my cameraman behind, I followed the designer.

"Jeanne! Great to see you!" he roared the moment he spotted me.

"I've missed you so much," I told him. "How have you been?"

"I've been okay," he said, dragging on his cigarette. "Wait till you see this show. An underwater fantasy . . . all about evolution! It goes really deep," he said with a hearty laugh. He was so excited to unveil his latest collection, and I got the sense he felt he'd outdone himself.

"Can't wait to see it!" I enthused.

"But how have *you* been?" he asked, looking me right in the eye. "Are you happy?"

I told him I was.

"Good, then," he said. "As long as you're happy. That's the most important thing."

The postshow reaction to McQueen's tour de force collection was exhilarating. Many felt he'd taken his genius to a whole new level. Things were looking bright for my designer friend.

Then, four months later, on the eve of his dear mother's funeral, McQueen hanged himself in his London home. I delivered the news to fans on *Fashion Television,* and honoring McQueen, I wore those fabulous little red boots, heart spilling over with sadness that one of the world's most beloved designers was gone.

McQueen was a true fashion hero but a vulnerable one. And I suppose it's precisely that vulnerability that humanized him. He wanted me to see that the price of success is sometimes pain and loneliness. I can't say the notion ever deterred me from pursuing my professional aspirations, but it did make me acutely aware of the fragility of those who create.

Though I haven't worn my red McQueen booties in years, they still occupy a special shelf in my closet, where I can see them every day. Beautifully crafted and so emblematic of edge and ebullience, this footwear is far from practical. Passion, drama, and vibrancy—these are qualities McQueen never lacked. I only wish he'd also found happiness, but it proved much more elusive to him than anything else.

Buttons & Bows

The fashion world is rife with paradoxes. For an industry famous for celebrating the notion of color, designers of color have often had a tough time getting the recognition they deserve. While things have certainly improved over the past couple of decades, the precious handful of wonderful Black talents entering the industry decades ago had to be tenacious and extraoriginal. Enter Patrick Kelly, the Mississippi-born designer who was the son of a home economics teacher and who began sewing in high school. His love of fashion led him to work after graduation in a thrift shop, where he started to upcycle garments and create his own designs. In 1979 he moved to New York, but still he struggled to gain a foothold in the industry.

Serendipitously, he met legendary model Pat Cleveland,

who encouraged him to move to Paris in 1980. Five years later, Kelly's couture clients included legendary luminaries from Bette Davis and Grace Jones to Goldie Hawn and Madonna. In 1987 the fashion conglomerate Warnaco invested in Kelly's business, and the following year he was admitted to the highly prestigious Chambre Syndicale—the first American ever to become a member of the organization.

At last Kelly's career was on fire, and when I met him around that time, I could fully understand why he'd been embraced so wholeheartedly by the fashion cognoscenti. He was utterly sweet, kind, and playful—a big kid decked out in ultrabaggy shorts, high-top sneakers, and a baseball cap. He was adamant about redefining racist imagery, using watermelon wedges, Black baby dolls, and golliwogs in his designs, and thereby reimagining them. He was also determined to celebrate women, regardless of their shape or size, a philosophy that was both inclusive and ahead of his time.

On *Fashion Television*'s first visit to his Paris studio, Kelly dressed me up in one of his sexy black minidresses, which featured a huge heart made of multicolored buttons across the chest. I adored the way this dress made me feel, and the love and upbeat positivity that this designer radiated were nothing short of intoxicating.

We took three of Kelly's gorgeous models out on the street in front of his studio, and he joyfully primped them as I conducted my interview. It made for one of the most fun encounters I'd ever had with a designer, and Kelly's warmth, enthusiasm, and charm totally floored me. Needless to say, we bonded. At the end of the afternoon, he lavished me with gifts: a vivid assortment of silk bows and buttons, all with little pins on the back so they could be worn as brooches. These were some of the most playful and spirited fashion accessories I could imagine, and thirty-five years later, the collection that Patrick Kelly presented me with is among my most treasured accessories.

The following year, 1989, Kelly came to Toronto, and we met up at a cool little Cajun restaurant for a chat. When I asked him about the demands of publicity since his career had skyrocketed, he said, "Who's going to buy these clothes if they don't know who we are?"

"So you're still the same old guy?" I asked.

He replied with a resounding "*Yes!*" And as I continued the interview, it became clear that it was the truth. He was exactly the same man I'd met years before, just a lot more famous now.

I asked Kelly if he felt like a real Parisian by now, after having lived in the City of Light for the past nine years.

"I'm still a southerner. I still open the door for women, it doesn't bother me. I try to say my grace before I eat, I pray before each show. . . . And I still like to have fun. I'm more funny than I am Parisian," he told me with a laugh.

I commented on the inspiring aura of love that seemed to be radiating from him and surrounding his whole team. "All the models love you, too," I told him. "Why is that so important for you?"

"I don't know," he said wistfully. "It's kind of that yanny-yanny, pink tofu, old leftover hippie, 'stop in the name of love' syndrome. But it works." He smiled then. "It really works."

I asked him if it was important to him to create clothes that make women feel good about themselves.

"You have to be proud," he said. "If you're big, if you're round, if you're skinny, if you're short. . . . If you come to me, you're definitely going to have a smile," he insisted.

Kelly's philosophy about body inclusivity was heartening and far ahead of its time. Yet it was only one aspect of the astounding success he was experiencing. His biggest contribution to fashion may well have been the fact that he was hell-bent on finding joy in a business often fraught with stress and seriousness.

"A lot of people think, 'Oh, if you're successful, you have to be serious.' Who needs it?" he said. "I just want to have some fun." Sadly, Patrick Kelly's irrepressible joie de vivre was short-lived: Ten months after saying this, in January 1990, Patrick Kelly succumbed to AIDS. He was thirty-five. The fashion world was shell-shocked to hear that we'd lost such a brilliant, unique, and promising talent. I couldn't help wondering whether the much-loved designer knew of his illness when we last saw each other on that cozy afternoon. Is that why his laughter was so infectious? Is that why I hear it in my mind to this day?

Heads Up

As glamorous and celebratory as hats have been in my wardrobe, there is one black denim newsboy cap that heralds an empowering style evolution for me. In July 2022, I'd just started chemotherapy treatments for breast cancer when the esteemed Canadian milliner David Dunkley had a lovely little black cap delivered to my door. It was the most thoughtful gesture: David knew it was only a matter of time before my hair would start falling out, and this wee chapeau offered a chic, practical solution. I was charmed both by his thoughtful gesture and by the style of the hat itself, so reminiscent of the mod caps of my youth, like the one John Lennon often wore.

But that style of cap had more personal connotations, too. It had been a favorite of my late mother's. She used to wear what she called a "kashket"—the type of felt cap worn by Hassidic little boys in the small Polish village where she grew up. As I held David's gift in my hands, I had to wonder: Was this a sign from my mother? Did she know about the physical ravages I was about to endure, and was she giving me the strength to endure them? I excitedly tried on the new cap and at once felt cool, cocky, and impish. I immediately knew this hat would see me through the months of disconcerting hair loss ahead.

A couple of weeks after the arrival of that first little hat, another exquisite newsboy cap arrived, this one courtesy of one of my dearest friends, the brilliant Irish designer Louise Kennedy. A vibrant shade of magenta, this stunning piece was made from a luxurious light wool fabric, with a fine sparkly thread running through it. It came with a matching, very elegant bomber jacket. I was floored by this gorgeous gift and incredulous that Louise had this "kashket"-style cap in her luxe collection.

So now I had a couple of these *au courant* caps—the black one, which I donned for everyday wear, and the smashing magenta one, which I wore with pride on special occasions, including for publicity shots for the Princess Margaret Cancer Centre campaign I starred in during the fall of 2022. There I was, larger than life, in my jaunty Louise Kennedy newsboy cap, on a gigantic electronic billboard in Toronto's busy Yonge and Dundas Square!

My precious hats have become constant reminders of the care and generosity of my designer friends, and proof positive that even when you're feeling out of sorts and insecure about the way you look, the right accessory can lift your spirits.

Thanks to the advancements of modern science, another kind

of headpiece became a staple during my weekly chemo treatments over the next three months. A company out of the UK called Paxman invented a kind of ice helmet that, if worn starting thirty minutes before the chemo infusions begin, can help a patient avoid hair loss. There were no guarantees, of course, and the rental of this "cooling cap" was rather costly, but I figured I'd make the investment and give it a try. Attempting to hang on to my hair was the least of my challenges, and I swore to myself that if I did lose it all, I'd wear my bald head like a badge of honor.

So, embracing my daunting situation, I took a few drops of CBD oil and a couple of extra-strength Tylenols, then put that dreaded ice helmet on a while before my first chemo treatment. It wasn't a very pleasant experience, but I still managed to find joy in posting photos of myself on Instagram wearing the ice helmet. "Ground control to Major Tom!" That was the caption on the first photo I posted. My sister dubbed the look "Space Age chic." The only attractive thing about that getup was having a playful attitude about it. And isn't that what determines great style anyway?

The first couple of weeks of treatment went rather swimmingly, and I seemed to be keeping all my hair. But around week four, it began to thin at a disconcerting rate. I'd wake up in the morning, lightly run my fingers through my hair, and countless strands would come right out. I was told to only brush my hair lightly to keep it in place, but my follicles had other plans. Every day, my beloved locks grew thinner and thinner.

I knew it was time to cut my hair shorter in anticipation of even more hair loss ahead. I contacted my dear hairstylist and friend Gregory Parvatan, who'd been styling my hair since 1979. He made a trip to my house to give me a cut.

"Oh, I've been wanting to give you a pixie for years!" Gregory admitted as he converted a corner of my dining room into a salon. "Short hair will look great on you!"

I knew Gregory's creative juices were flowing, and he was eager to get me out of my trademark long bangs and blunt cut.

"I'm not ready for a pixie cut yet," I protested. "Let's just do a shorter, more manageable bob."

"Anything you say, love," said Gregory.

That's one of the many things I adore about Gregory. Besides being a master technician with scissors, he never imposes his aesthetic, unlike some other hairstylists I've known who are constantly trying to talk you into things.

Still, I wept as I went through this hairstyle transformation. I knew it was only a matter of time before more of my hair would fall out and I'd have to crop it even shorter. Somehow, this was a loss that I could see and name, and I poured out my grief in that moment because life as I knew it was changing forever.

Sometimes, it's important just to get it out. I cried for a while as Gregory did my hair. And then, once I was done crying, I was done. I tried to look on the bright side. I was losing my hair, but in a few weeks, I'd begin a new fashion adventure—wearing hats of all kinds to get me through the tough stuff. Not only would people be seeing me in a new way but I'd be seeing the world in a new way, too. And maybe, that would be a good thing.

Purple Haze

While showing off one's baby bump via form-fitting clothes has become a proud and bold way for expectant moms to dress, as I've mentioned, it was a different story back in the eighties, when I went through my two pregnancies. I shake my head when I recall some of the garments I wore while pregnant—but perhaps none were as cringeworthy as the oversized sparkly purple pullover I wore the night I was serenaded by the late Canadian folk legend Gordon Lightfoot.

Scoring an interview with the gentle and brilliant Gordon was never easy, but I was set on featuring him on *The NewMusic*. Because Gordon was famous for his reluctance to be interviewed, in 1982, to coincide with the release of his album *Shadows,* Warner Brothers and his management company issued an interview album to radio stations titled *Lightfoot Talks Shadows*. On the album Lightfoot answered questions that journalists had asked in advance. Upon receiving the strange interview record, my spirited producer, John Martin, decided conducting an interview with the elusive and not physically present Gordon while spinning vinyl would make for hilarious TV. So, for my first Gordon Lightfoot interview, I sat in a studio with a record player only, asking my invisible guest questions that were answered every time I put the needle to the record.

"So, Gordon, what kinds of music fans do you think really embrace the music that you offer?" I asked, trying my hardest not to laugh before placing the needle on the appropriate answer track.

"Our particular audience is a very, very nice kind of people. We don't have any 'yahoos' hanging around," Gordon replied.

I then lifted the needle, getting ready to place it on the next track.

"And with all your success, one would have thought that you'd have moved stateside by now. Why didn't you ever move down to the States?" I asked.

"Uh, this is gonna sound kinda phony, but I really like Toronto a lot. . . . I like my city and I like going canoeing."

I nodded knowingly at the turntable. It took all my strength not to laugh out loud.

The whole "interview" was completely preposterous, but it did make for a few minutes of entertaining and irreverent TV. My only hope was that Gordon wouldn't hate us for it.

A few days after the silly segment aired, I got a call from Gordon's manager, Bernie Fiedler.

"Jeanne, Gordon saw the piece," he said.

I held my breath, certain that our revered Canadian idol was going to be outraged.

"He thought it was really amusing. I know how important your show is. And I'm trying to get Gordon to do more TV interviews. But it's tough. Anyway, just wanted to let you know that we appreciate you."

I was gobsmacked. Seriously? Gordon was a better sport than I ever could have imagined. And I breathed a huge sigh of relief.

It wasn't until 1986 that I was finally granted an actual interview with Gordon for our show. My crew and I were invited to his home. I was so happy to finally sit down with this humble genius, and evidently, as reluctant as he may have been to do on-camera interviews, he was relaxed in our company. He even pulled out his guitar to play a few snippets of songs! It made for great TV. A couple of months after the interview aired, I got another call from Bernie.

"That was a great piece, Jeanne! Gordon loved doing the interview with you. Sure took us a while to get him to do it, eh?" He laughed. "Thanks for being so patient. And to say thank you, he'd like to take you out to dinner."

I couldn't believe it. I was elated. "Oh, wow, Bernie, that is amazing! I'd love to have dinner with Gordon. How kind of him!" I gushed.

"Okay, let's make it for next week. Gordon will meet you at George Bigliardi's."

Dining at the famous George Bigliardi's steak house with the iconic Gordon . . . Was this real? As much of a fantasy as the notion was, I couldn't help feeling a bit odd about being six months pregnant and not exactly feeling like a cool female rock reporter. I immediately started thinking about what I'd wear, though I knew all my hip clothes were pretty much out of the question with my burgeoning belly.

The evening of the dinner, I opted to team my new maternity jeans with an oversized sparkly purple pullover. It was just before Christmas, so I figured a little glitz might seem suitably festive. More important, though, the sweater was roomy enough to disguise my significant baby bump, not that it was some big secret. People close to me knew, but I most definitely hadn't announced anything publicly. And remember, this was the mideighties when we pregnant gals weren't strutting our baby bumps with as much pride as we ought to have because we were all afraid of losing our jobs—a real possibility at the time!

I wasn't nuts about my purple sweater—not at all—but at least it didn't look like the typical dowdy maternity fare.

I arrived at Bigliardi's with the excitement of a schoolgirl but tried to act my coolest.

"I'm meeting Gordon Lightfoot here," I said nonchalantly to the maître d' and was escorted to the bar. Gordon jumped to his feet the minute he saw me. And if I was a tad uncomfortable, he immediately put me at ease.

"Well, hi, Jeanne," he smoothly drawled. "Really appreciate that you could join me tonight."

"Thank you so much for the invitation, Gordon. So sweet of you."

"I just wanted to say thank you for giving me all that publicity . . . even though I'd been playing hard to get for all those years." He laughed then, a wonderful sound.

We took our seats on the barstools and continued our friendly conversation. I was wondering if Gordon had noticed that I was pregnant under my big sparkly sweater. Maybe he just thought I'd put on weight? I was about to tell him when a familiar face appeared in the restaurant. Dini Petty was my Citytv colleague, the popular coanchor of the six o'clock news and someone with whom I often shared the anchor desk when I was reporting on entertainment. She looked completely shocked to see me sitting at the bar with Gordon Lightfoot.

"Hey, darling!" she cooed. "I just heard your great news! Can I touch your belly for good luck?" she asked.

"Oh wow! Congratulations!" Gordon chimed in. "That's wonderful!"

As soon as Dini left, Gordon and I launched into a discussion about the importance of family and how exciting it was that my life was about to change. He had three kids at the time and was so proud of them all.

We had a wonderful dinner that night, and I just kept thinking how surreal the whole thing was, to be sitting beside the awesome Gordon Lightfoot having dinner at the bar like a couple of old pals.

"Hey, let's go back to my place," Gordon suggested as we got up to leave. Of course, if that came from any other musician who had crossed my path at any other time, I might have balked. But this was definitely *not* a come-on. Gordon was such a gentleman. And so I agreed.

"But I have an early morning tomorrow, so I'll just pop in for a few minutes."

We came up the driveway of his big, storied mansion in Rosedale. I felt like I was in a dream. I'd been to his house before with my TV crew in tow, but this time was different.

"Can I get you anything to drink?" Gordon asked as he showed me into the living room.

"No, I'm okay. Where should I sit?"

"I usually just sit on the floor!" he said with a laugh.

I plopped myself down on the rug, and strangely, I don't think I've ever felt more comfortable.

There was Gordon, getting out his guitar, and before I knew it, he was sitting on the floor across from me, asking me what I wanted to hear.

I had so many favorite Lightfoot songs but blurted out, "If You Could Read My Mind."

Gordon launched into the most exquisite rendition of that tune, singing and playing so sweetly and so perfectly that my heart melted. I knew this was his way of saying thank you.

I was enchanted, and as I sat there in my big, sparkly purple sweater with my hands on my belly, I was quite certain that my baby could hear the beautiful music, too.

Gone Fishing

I've always been a big fan of fishnet hose. I first started wearing them in the sixties. Back then I always went for white ones because light-colored, textured hosiery was very mod and on trend. But by the time the eighties rolled around, hosiery trends had changed, and the playful vamp in me developed a penchant for dark fishnet stockings.

Beyond fashion, black fishnets spoke of glam and daring. Anytime I wanted to make a bit of a sexy statement, I'd brazenly don a pair of black fishnets to give my outfit a bit of oomph. That's exactly what I did one night when I was slated to attend the McMichael Gallery's Moonlight Gala in 2015, an event that I was dreading. But by donning my fishnets, I changed everything.

By this point, I was sixty-three. I'd been married twice and divorced twice. I'd been in and out of a few relationships, and I just hadn't managed to find "the one"—a soulmate who was right for me. Meanwhile, my mum was ninety-four and totally obsessed with me finding somebody to share my life with.

"Jeanne, it's not good to be alone," she constantly reminded me. "Why can't you find somebody?"

"Mum, it's not that simple," I'd repeat to her for the five millionth time. "I'd love to be in a relationship as much as you'd love it for me, but it's hard meeting the right guy."

She'd shake her head then as if nothing made sense. There was no explaining to her that at my age—at any age, for that matter—it wasn't exactly easy to find a match.

Sometimes, instead of talking to me directly about my matelessness, she'd talk to others around me, pretending I wasn't there. "I just can't understand why Jeanne can't find a guy," she would lament to her caregiver on the way home from dinner at my house every Friday night. "I feel like I have to hang on until she finds someone," she'd say with a big sigh.

"Mum, you know I can hear you, right?" I'd tell her, but it was as if I hadn't spoken.

By this point in my mother's long life, her health was failing. In many ways, she felt ready to go—to leave this world for whatever waited beyond. But the fact that I was on my own was so worrisome to her—and it worried me, too, because I knew she was hanging on for me. She used to pray every day that I'd find a partner, always adding that she needed this to happen sooner rather than later.

As for my feelings on the matter, I was at a stage in my life

HEART ON MY SLEEVE

where I felt okay being by myself. I had a pretty fabulous life, single though I was. Why should I stress about being alone, maybe even for the rest of my life? Was that really so bad? I was happy, financially stable, and fulfilled . . . Still, my life philosophy was always to maintain an open mind and an open heart. So, that's what I did. I remained open to the idea of finding somebody, but there was no way I was going to be desperate about it.

In May 2015, despite her efforts to hang on until I found a partner, my beloved mum succumbed to the ravages of Parkinson's disease. My heart was broken. She'd been such a good mum for so long, and the thought of her not being there was so painful. She'd always said that even if she was gone, she'd still be there for me, and I took solace in that, hoping she was right. I'd lost my mother in the concrete world, but I tried to take comfort in the idea that she now looked over me as a guardian angel.

At the reception after her funeral, as I stood on my backyard deck greeting visitors, a cardinal sang brightly from a tree in the yard. Its scarlet plumage, its relentless song—was this her? Was she watching over me?

Two weeks after my mother's passing, I was supposed to attend a gala fundraiser at the McMichael Art Gallery in Kleinburg, Ontario, about forty-five minutes outside Toronto. The McMichael, with its beautiful woodland setting, is a wonderful Canadian gallery, and driving out there on a Sunday afternoon had always been one of my mum's favorite outings. But Mum was gone, and she wasn't coming back. Even though I'd been named an honorary patron of the event, I was not excited about attending. My heart still felt so heavy with grief.

– 121 –

When Diane Wilson, one of the board members, called, I told her how I was feeling.

"Diane, I'd love to go, honestly, but my mother just died and I'm not really feeling up to it. Besides," I continued, "I don't have a date!" I laughed then, hoping to lighten the mood a little.

The truth was, I couldn't stand the idea of donning a little black dress and attending yet another gala soirée when I was feeling more alone than ever.

"Oh, come on, Jeanne," Diane said. "It'll be good for you! You don't have to bring a date. Just bring a friend. We'd so love to have you there," she pleaded.

"I'll think about it," I said. And I did.

A couple of days before the event, I mentioned it to my bestie, Penny Fiksel. Penny and I had been close since we were eleven years old, and she was almost as eager as my mum to see me settled and happy with someone.

"That sounds like great fun," she said. "I love the McMichael. You really should go."

"Really not into it," I explained. "Another black cocktail dress, another swish affair. Another date where I'm dateless."

"I'll be your date!" Penny suggested. "You know how much your mother loved the McMichael. This will be our tribute to her. Let's hire a limo and go together. It'll be so much fun. I've never even been there before!"

As reluctant as I was, Penny has always been persistent. By the time I got off the phone, I had agreed to go to the Moonlight Gala with my friend. Maybe she was right. Maybe it would be good for me to get out. And spending time with Penny was always a treat.

This meant it was little black dress time. And I had several to choose from, so I had no excuses. Maybe it was because I knew I had to shake my case of the blues that I chose to go the playful route, donning my Lida Baday cocktail dress, with its short, tight, sequined skirt. To punch things up, I added a pair of black fishnet tights—and teamed the outfit with a pair of sparkly black platform stilettos. As I looked in the mirror, I felt at once transformed and empowered. I imagined my mum behind me, nodding her approval at my outfit. I knew she wouldn't want me to mope. She wanted me to live life to the fullest, to be happy. And so, to honor her, I would try to do just that.

Penny and I got into our limo that night and were driven out to the event. Within minutes of arriving, she was off chatting up some guests while I did my obligatory posing for photographers. By the time I was done, my "date" had totally disappeared.

I shoulda known. I sighed to myself as I picked up a flute of bubbly from a dapper server and retreated to a couch near the bar. Why had I gotten all dressed up and rented a limo to go all the way to Kleinburg? To hang out at a party by myself?

No sooner had the thought crossed my mind than I caught the eye of a man across the room. He was a silver-haired gentleman with a goatee. I noticed right away that he was wearing a sharp gray suit. His eyes didn't waver—they remained glued to mine. Was he checking me out? Before I could answer that question, the attractive man made a beeline for me and was suddenly standing in front of me with an outstretched hand.

"Hi, my name is Iain MacInnes," he said with a bright smile.

I gazed into his blue eyes for a moment, not sure what to say.

"I'm on the foundation board of the McMichael, and I just wanted to congratulate you on your career. I've always admired you for having kept yourself so relevant."

I was floored. I couldn't believe what he'd just said. If there was anything I wanted to hear, that was it! I'd been dancing as fast as I could, working so hard to remain relevant in my profession, and here was a man who had forgone all the niceties and suddenly complimented me on the thing that mattered the most to me at the time. Also, he was supercute, and there was an energy coming from him that was nothing short of captivating.

It took me a moment to recover, but eventually I said, "Thank you so much for saying that. And thank you for noticing."

"How could I not?" he replied.

We launched into a spirited conversation, and a few minutes later, Penny appeared.

"Oh, I see you've met," she said. "Jeanne, Iain lost his wife last year. Iain, Jeanne just lost her mother."

That's Penny—she tells it like it is. But of course, I knew she was trying to convey something else to me and me alone.

As it turned out, Penny knew a lot about this handsome stranger. For a moment, I wondered why, but it then became clear that she'd been chatting with him and his gorgeous sister, Sandie, when we first arrived. Iain had explained to Penny that this was the first big social event he'd attended as a widower, and it was only because of his sister's coaxing that he'd complied. I can just imagine what Penny must have said in response.

A few minutes after joining our conversation, Penny left us to our own devices, and within about fifteen minutes of our meeting, I'd learned so much about Iain. He was a financial adviser and a stockbroker, originally from Scotland, who'd been living in London, Ontario. But when his wife died after a lengthy illness, he'd moved to nearby Port Stanley, a small beach town on the shore of Lake Erie. He had three lovely daughters, all in their twenties, from his first marriage. He adored art and Motown music. And he regularly traveled to Scotland to visit family.

"I love to travel. Do you, Jeanne?" he asked.

"Oh, I do," I replied. I explained how much I loved Ireland and how I went there often to spend time with dear friends.

"There's nothing like friends. And family," he said.

"I agree," I replied.

We kept talking, and everything was so easy with him, so open and free. I was loving his sense of humor, his engaging chatter. It felt like a window had just opened and I was getting an exhilarating blast of fresh air. The electricity between us was unmistakable, too. Several times we were interrupted by other partygoers, and while Iain left my side occasionally over the course of the evening, he always returned, eager to chat more and ready to pick up exactly where we'd left off.

At one point, when he found his way back to me, he popped an important question.

"Do you ever think that maybe you'd go to dinner with me sometime?" he asked sheepishly, as if he doubted I'd say yes.

"Oh, of course. That would really be nice," I enthused, and I meant it.

That night we exchanged email addresses and phone numbers. Then we posed together for a photo before we said our goodbyes.

In the limo on the way home, I couldn't wipe the smile off my face.

"Isn't he just the cutest?" Penny said. "He's such a great guy, Jeanne!"

I agreed with her, but in my head, I wondered: Would he really call me?

We were about halfway home when my phone dinged. It was a text from Iain.

Would you like to go to Scotland with me?

he asked.

I couldn't believe my eyes. I had to read it twice to make sure I wasn't missing something. It was a wild and crazy proposal considering the fact that we'd just met.

"Penny, you won't believe this," I said. "Check this out!" I showed her Iain's text. "What should I say?"

"Say you'll go!" she immediately shot back.

And I don't know why I felt so confident, but I did. I typed a single-word answer:

Absolutely.

Then I pressed send.

A week later, Iain took the train to Toronto, and we went on our first date. We had a lovely dinner at a quaint French restaurant, and after, we decided to go for a walk. We stopped by my house so I could change into a pair of comfy shoes and get my dog, Gus.

As we strolled through Yorkville, we came across a small club where we could hear a live band playing through the wide-open doors. We tied Gus up outside where we could watch him and popped into the club for a quick drink. When the band launched into an Earth, Wind & Fire tune, Iain asked me to dance. I slid off my barstool, and for the first time in a long time, I danced not alone but with him. We haven't stopped dancing since.

When I traveled to Scotland with Iain a few weeks after that date and stayed with his amazing relatives, I felt as though I'd come home. It was like meeting long-lost family. But most profoundly, I knew with all of my heart that my mum had sent this man to me. She couldn't wait any longer for him to arrive, but somehow, she guided him to me.

Iain is everything she would have wanted for her daughter. We often talk about that first magical night of our meeting. I tell him how he won me with his disarming compliment, his open heart, and his big smile. And he tells me how he saw me across the room in my little black dress and fishnets, and how something compelled him to walk over to meet me.

Something indeed—the gentle nudge of my angelic, match-making mum.

Fancy Pants

While so many of the celebrities I've interviewed over the years have powerhouse personae, many are hiding their inner vulnerability. It's understandable when you think of all the pressure they're under to live up to their reputations. Celebrities often appear to be larger than life and practically superhuman. But there's always a raw heart that beats within.

I have a particularly cherished pair of black velvet trousers in my wardrobe that I haven't worn in over twenty years—but they conjure a bittersweet memory of the time I interviewed one of the strongest imagemakers of our time, Madonna.

In 1992 I splurged on an outrageously dramatic, voluminous pair of black velvet bell bottoms by famed New York designer Anna Sui. She was and continues to be much-loved among young women craving a bohemian spirit in their style. Back in the nineties, Anna Sui was a go-to label for models and pop stars alike—and her Soho boutique was a style mecca for many, including Naomi Campbell.

A few weeks after making my big purchase, I was invited, as host of *MovieTelevision,* to interview Madonna at a New York press junket. The pop star had a new film coming out—*Body of Evidence*—a noir thriller about a killer who uses her body as a deadly sexual weapon. I was ecstatic to finally have a chance to sit down with the icon who'd captured everyone's imagination, and though I was promised only four minutes with her, I vowed to make them count.

I prepared for the interview as best I could, and when it came to the question of what to wear for this auspicious occasion, I immediately thought of my new Anna Sui bell-bottoms. Besides having the right theatrical flare, these fabulous pants were designed by one of Madonna's favorite American designers. No doubt Madonna would be impressed by my taste and style.

I paired the bell-bottoms with an olive-green shirt with billowing sleeves and a paisley vest. The whole outfit gave off a cool vintage vibe that I hoped was both on trend and chic. After all, when you only have precious seconds to establish rapport, you'd better look your best.

On the eve of the interviews, the invited press attended a special screening of the movie. The theater was packed with press and regular moviegoers alike, everyone eager to see Madonna in her first dramatic role. But as the film began to play out on the big screen, the hoots and hollers got louder and louder. Let's just say the audience wasn't happy.

Madonna looked very beautiful on-screen, but as the late, great film critic Roger Ebert said in his review, "I've seen comedies with fewer laughs than *Body of Evidence,* and this is a movie that isn't even trying to be funny." Ouch. As I sat there cringing between mouthfuls of popcorn, I could only hope that Madonna wasn't in the house witnessing this painful reception.

The next morning, I headed to the Manhattan hotel where the interviews were taking place. I wasn't sure how I was going to congratulate this superstar on a movie that was not well received, but I was still excited to meet her. I entered the designated suite hoping that Madonna and I would get along famously. After all, I was wearing my fabulous Anna Sui bell-bottoms, and surely she'd appreciate them.

As I sashayed in, I spotted Madonna, dressed all in black, sitting in a straight-back chair, three cameras surrounding her. She was much tinier than I'd imagined, and from the look on her face, she wasn't in a particularly good mood.

There was no time to waste. "Hi, I'm Jeanne Beker," I said to the PA standing by.

"Hey, cool pants!" one of the cameramen called out.

"Thanks," I said, thrilled that my trousers had been noticed. Madonna turned her head to look at me.

"Hi, great to see you, Madonna," I said, trying to muster all the warmth I could as I settled into the chair across from her.

That's when my heart skipped a beat. Madonna was wearing the exact same black velvet bell-bottoms.

"How funny!" I said. "We're wearing exactly the same pants."

"Oh, are we?" she replied. She did not look amused.

"Yeah. Anna Sui. I was just in her shop last week."

Madonna was silent. I realized we were wasting valuable time, so I launched into the interview.

"What excites you the most about acting in front of the camera?"

"Getting to play another person," she replied. "Getting to be someone else, besides me, I guess."

"How much of a persona do you feel the real Madonna has become in the eyes of the public, as opposed to who you may really be?"

"How close is the image with me?" she asked. "Not very, because at this point, people's opinions of me and the stories that have spun out of control about me are so not true that, well . . . how could anyone possibly really know me and know who I am?"

I never forgot that answer, or the fact that Madonna spent the rest of that afternoon explaining herself, over and over again, trying to let people know that there was far more to her than met the eye. She wanted people to know she wasn't just her image— she was someone else entirely, and we would never know her.

In the end, I felt bad that I may have upstaged her with my choice of clothing. It wasn't intentional, but my choice of Anna Sui and the exact same pants had created a rift between us instead of the proximity I'd hoped for. After all, how can you be a true original when the interviewer sitting right across from you is wearing the same pants?

Nevertheless, I've never gotten rid of those Anna Sui bell-bottoms. I've tried letting them go, but at the last moment, I always find myself putting them back in my closet. Maybe it's that I cherish the memory of an awkward but revealing moment. Or maybe I keep them as a reminder that no matter the power of a garment to help us feel a certain way, no piece of clothing is ever who we really are.

Ballet Slippers

Physical performance has always been a passion of mine, ever since I got my first pair of ballet slippers at the age of five. Every Saturday morning I would stuff those precious black slippers, along with a tiny black leotard, into a sweet little blue carrying case with red velvety lambs embossed on it—a birthday gift from my sister—and I'd fantasize about becoming a prima ballerina as I proudly rode the streetcar to my weekly ballet lesson. But my dreams were crushed before I even finished my first year when I began to develop cramping in my upper legs.

"It must be those ballet classes she's been going to," my pediatrician, Dr. Slavens, deduced.

"Oy!" exclaimed my mother, realizing her own dreams for me were about to be crushed as well. "Okay, I guess she'll have to quit."

I'll never forget the day she broke the news to me. My mother was deflated, but I was devastated. In retrospect, I think my cramps were likely due to the unconventional way I'd splay my legs while sitting on the floor in my kindergarten classroom, but at the time, I hadn't figured that out. At any rate, much to my dismay, I never was able to pursue my childhood dancing dreams, though I always harbored the urge to communicate through movement and to study some kind of physical discipline.

In 1973, while I was studying theater performance at York University, I became intrigued with the art of mime, a dramatic form of corporeal expression that appealed to me greatly because in mime, either you create the illusion or you don't. There could be nothing half-assed about it. I had a tremendous amount of respect for all the discipline required to perfect the technique. I took some classes from a Toronto mime named Paul Gaulin and learned that his teacher was an old man in Paris named Étienne Decroux, who was known as the father of modern mime. Decroux had taught the great French actor-director Jean Louis Barrault and the famed Marcel Marceau himself. Even David Bowie had studied with Decroux. I knew I had to learn from this master, and I began plotting and planning a move to Paris.

I wrote to Decroux a few weeks before my planned departure, telling him I was eager to enroll in his classes, which were held in the basement of his small home in the Bois de Boulogne on the outskirts of Paris. Though I got a discouraging letter from his wife about a week before my departure date saying his classes were all full, I decided it was too late to change my plans. I flew to Paris nonetheless. I made my way out to Decroux's home, knocked on his door, and pleaded with Madame Decroux in my very broken high school French.

"*C'est quelque chose qui est très important pour moi,*" I whined to the matronly lady in the floral apron at the door. It's something very important to me.

"*Désolée, ma chérie,* it's not possible," she said, trying to shut me down.

"But I've come so far to be here," I said in French. "Please . . ." And then I began to cry.

"I'm sorry. There's nothing I can do," she replied as she shook her head. "But give me your name and write down your address in Paris." She handed me a paper and a pen.

I wrote *Jeanne Beker* and the name of my little hotel on the Left Bank. I handed the paper and pen back to her.

She read what I'd written, and suddenly, her eyes lit up. "*Jeanne?*" she said, pronouncing it the French way. "That's my name, too!"

She looked me up and down, then seemed to change her mind. "Okay, Jeanne. Come on Friday. You'll start your studies with Monsieur Decroux then," she said as her face broke into a smile.

"Really?" I asked. I was incredulous at her change of heart and thanked her profusely.

I left practically skipping down the street. The next day I went to Paris's legendary dance gear shop Repetto and purchased a brand-new pair of black leather ballet slippers. I hadn't been so excited about footwear since receiving my first ballet slippers. I couldn't wait to start my studies with the grand master.

Friday came, and my first class with the master of mime took place as expected. It was exhilarating and inspiring. Gathered in the studio was a small international cast of students, including an affable fellow Torontonian named Charlie Gundy. He was tall and lanky, with superbly thick, curly dark hair, and he wore wire-rim aviator glasses. He had the wonderful kind of face that made you want to smile—like some character from the commedia del l'arte. Most important, he was kind and warm to me, the new-comer, and since he'd already been studying with Decroux for about a year, he took me under his wing.

Charlie and I became fast friends, and after a while he invited me to dinner at his small shared apartment in the Bastille area. It was a sixth-floor walk-up, with a shared toilet at the end of a long dark hallway. That "toilet" was nothing more than a huge hole in the floor. It became clear to me that Charlie was living in pretty dismal conditions, yet I respected him for "suffering for his art."

That first Christmas, I was missing my boyfriend, Marty, back in Toronto. Charlie was planning on flying back for the holidays to visit his parents, and he offered to take a gift to Marty for me. We went on a Christmas shopping spree, and I found just the right present. I sent it back to Toronto with Charlie and asked Marty and my best friend, Penny, to retrieve the gift at Charlie's parents' house.

Penny contacted me after completing the mission. "Oh my Lord, Jeanne! Who is this Charlie Gundy guy? Marty and I freaked out when we pulled up to his parents' home in Forest Hill!"

"What do you mean?" I asked.

"His parents live in a freaking mansion! Actually, it looks more like a castle! Marty was so intimidated. He started fantasizing about a showdown with Charlie over you. So this Charlie is just a friend, right?"

"Yes, just a dear friend. Marty has nothing to worry about," I said. But I was as amazed as Penny to discover that Charlie came from wealth yet was living in virtual poverty in Paris.

As it turns out, Charlie's grandfather was the cofounder of Wood Gundy, one of Canada's leading securities and investment firms. His father had worked his way up from mail clerk to become chairman of the board of the mighty company. But dear Charlie had opted to live an artist's humble life, far away from the lavish trappings of his family's fortune. That surprising discovery endeared him to me even more, and I held on to my own simple ballet slippers all the more tightly, determined that if I was going to make it as an artist, I would do it on my own steam as well.

All these years later, my very first pair of ballet slippers, along with my tiny black leotard, hang in a gilded picture frame in my upstairs hallway. It was my mum who preserved those precious vestiges of my childhood in that way. They serve as a constant reminder of my mother's belief in me, and the undying passion for performance art that's stayed with me throughout the years. These precious mementos also remind me of that big artistic dream I pursued in Paris, when Charlie was my tour guide and showed me that the pursuit of artistry often involves sacrifice.

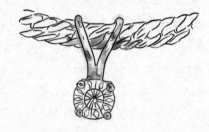

Diamond in the Rough

My father always held diamonds in high esteem. He saw them not only as symbols of luxury but as emblems of success. I remember his excitement when he presented my mother with a small but elegant diamond ring for her fortieth birthday in 1960. And in 1982, for my thirtieth birthday, he gave me a 0.5 carat diamond pendant on a beautiful gold chain. It was the first diamond I'd ever owned, and it was a precious token of love from my dad. It also became mine at a time when I was finding success in my career, and somehow, all the sparkle seemed like a harbinger of what was in store for me as I rubbed shoulders with some of the greatest cultural icons of our times.

I'd always been in awe of one of those luminaries in particular: Leonard Cohen. I became enthralled by him when my hip and savvy sister brought home a copy of *Beautiful Losers* in 1966, long before Cohen launched his career as a singer-songwriter. Every cool woman at the time seemed to be crushing on this handsome and powerful Montreal writer. The fact that he was Canadian and Jewish made him doubly appealing to me. There was something familiar and accessible about him, though his wildly romantic lifestyle on some Greek island was light-years away from my suburban teenage life. With every new Leonard Cohen poem I read, my reverence for his artistry grew. *Energy of Slaves,* published in 1971, was one of the most beautiful books I'd ever read.

When I moved to Paris in 1973, I was delighted to discover what huge fans my new French friends were of Leonard's music, which was often the soundtrack for our weekend jaunts to the countryside. A decade later, when I was working at Citytv as host of *The NewMusic* and entertainment reporter for the nightly news, I befriended an earnest young man who came to work for Citytv president, Moses Znaimer. His name was Barrie Wexler, and he had recently moved to Toronto from Montreal, where he'd been involved in a host of artistic endeavors.

Barrie let it be known that he was a close pal of Leonard Cohen's, which I found most impressive. When Barrie learned of my close friendship with Canadian skating legend and artist Toller Cranston, his creative cogs started turning.

"Hey, Jeanne, Leonard's coming to town and we'd love it if you could introduce us to Toller. I want to produce a TV musical featuring Leonard, kind of a video album, and I think Toller could play an important part in it."

I'd told Barrie about the exotic salons Toller regularly hosted in his living room—performance extravaganzas featuring poetry readings and solo dance recitals by the likes of Toronto's brilliant performer Robert Desrosiers.

"You're not thinking about a skating special, are you?" I asked.

"No. Nothing like that. I want to cast Toller in some kind of dramatic role, and maybe he'd help us access some of the amazing dancers he's friends with," Barrie explained. "I need your help in showing Leonard a handful of music videos. He isn't really familiar with the genre. And I'll give you an associate producer credit."

Watching music videos with Leonard Cohen? Let's just say Barrie didn't have to ask me twice.

A couple of weeks later, Toller hosted one of his late-night salons, at which he served the usual fancy strawberry desserts and champagne. I invited Barrie and told him to bring Leonard along.

Toller's living room, on the second floor of his Cabbagetown home, was a kind of colorful Victorian parlor. Every square inch of wall space featured an eclectic array of Canadian artists. Rich oriental carpets covered the floor, and in the middle of the room was a huge Venetian glass fountain. By the time I arrived, the party was in full swing. I made a beeline to where Barrie and Leonard were sitting, sipping on champagne.

"I see you two have already been initiated," I said with a laugh. "And I gather you've already met our host."

"Yes, we have. Leonard, this is Jeanne. And, Jeanne, meet Leonard."

Suddenly, the whole surreal scene became even more elevated, with the charming and impossibly handsome Leonard offering me a warm smile and an even warmer welcome.

"I'm really looking forward to our video-viewing session tomorrow," my suave, soft-spoken hero said.

"Yeah, me too!" I replied enthusiastically.

A little later Desrosiers danced, and after, we discussed the idea of him and Toller working on the Leonard Cohen video album. Of course, Toller was very excited by this possible collaboration and suggested that his beautiful dancer friend Anne Ditchburn and cofounder of the National Ballet Celia Franca, could also be part of the production.

The next day I met Leonard at Citytv, and together we viewed stacks of videos by the Clash, A Flock of Seagulls, Blondie, Talking Heads, and even Michael Jackson. Leonard was enthralled by this relatively new medium, excited that he would soon have a video offering of his own—albeit in the form of a half-hour special.

"I'd like to thank you for the screening session, Jeanne," he said when we were done. "Will you have lunch with me tomorrow?"

That was an offer I couldn't refuse.

Leonard was staying at the Windsor Arms Hotel, and just around the corner, on Bloor Street West, was a popular lunch spot, a Danish restaurant called the Copenhagen Room. It was there that we met for our casual meal. I arrived a few minutes early and waited for the legendary Leonard—my lunch date—to appear.

On time, he strolled in, wearing a charcoal coat and looking as handsome as ever. "So, tell me about your life," he said as he sat down.

"Oh, it's a busy one. But I love what I do, and so many amazing doors keep opening for me."

"And how's your love life?"

I couldn't believe he was asking, but that was Leonard—he preferred real conversations to small talk.

"Well, round about now," I said, "my love life is pretty good, but I've sure had some bumps in the road. You know, sometimes, love hurts."

He smiled knowingly, and I suddenly felt a little silly philosophizing about love to this grand master of love poetry.

I can't remember much of our conversation, only that I was enraptured by this warm, gentle, curious man sitting across from me. It was hard to believe he was also the passionate, fiery artist who wrote so intimately about lust, pain, and longing.

I next saw Leonard a couple of months later on the set of the video production for *I Am a Hotel* at Toronto's King Edward Hotel. He was as affable as ever. The half-hour video revolved around the relationships of a small cast of fictional characters who were guests or employees at a hotel. Leonard sang a total of five songs, including his hit "Suzanne." He played the part of a spirit who'd inhabited the hotel for years, observing all the goings-on. Toller played the hotel's manager; Robert Desrosiers played a bellhop; Anne Ditchburn, a cheating wife; and Celia Franca, a diva. The video won a Golden Rose international TV award at the Montreux TV Festival in 1984.

When Leonard's poetry compilation *Book of Mercy* came out

that same year, I had the chance to do a sit-down interview with him at which he signed my copy of his book: "For Jeanne—the Queen of Questions . . . From your admirer, Leonard." Not surprisingly, I melted.

A few months later Leonard was back in Toronto, this time for a swish party at the home of local art dealer Arij Gasiunasen, which I attended wearing a chic little black dress, subtly accessorized with the precious gift my father had given me. Leonard spotted me in the backyard of the lavish home, where he was smoking a cigarette. He greeted me as if I were an old friend.

"Hey, you! How've you been, darlin'?" he asked.

"Oh, good," I said as I toyed with my diamond pendant. "Hanging in. You know, just trying to dance as fast as I can."

He smiled. "Well, it all looks great on you. Just make sure you leave some time for fun."

That was the last encounter I had with Leonard, but it was a good one, and his parting words were wise ones. I left that party feeling so lucky to know him. To me, he was a jewel of a man, as clear, brilliant, and beautiful as any diamond.

My family in 1952, featuring baby me. It was the same year my dad managed to buy our first home, which he turned into a rooming house in order to pay the mortgage.

In the backyard of our Toronto home with my sister, Marilyn, and Mum. We were always well dressed in those early years, thanks to the hand-me-downs we regularly received from our well-heeled American cousins.

My mother's family in Kozowa, Poland, in 1938, just before the war broke out. My seventeen-year-old mum is standing between my grandparents, in the center of the photo. She was the only one in the family who survived the Holocaust.

LEFT: My parents, Bronia and Joseph, in 1945. They lived a monumental love story. It was my father's motto of "Don't be afraid. And never give up!" that helped see them through the war.

BELOW: My parents in Lodz, Poland, shortly after the war, determined to rebuild their shattered lives.

My dad always encouraged my mum to turn up the style volume. This custom velvet gown with its mink collar was inspired by a designer creation my dad had spotted in *Vogue*.

I was beyond excited in 1955, when this pony showed up at our house for a photo shoot. I was so proud of the dressy little outfit I wore.

I always looked up to my sister, Marilyn, who constantly helped inspire my imagination.

My sister, Marilyn, was the personification of cool. My mother made this corduroy zebra-print dress for her in the sixties, which went perfectly with her go-go boots.

I was especially proud of the sparkly dress and matching booties I wore to my Sweet Sixteen in 1968, inspired by an outfit I saw on the cover of *Harper's Bazaar*.

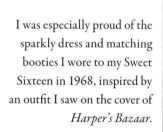

ABOVE: Studying mime in Paris in 1973–74 was such an inspiring time for me. I was intrigued by the pure magic of communication without words, without costume.

ABOVE RIGHT: My very first headshot was taken in 1968, and I was adamant about projecting a sense of whimsy in my floppy felt hat. *Photo by Mike Gluss*

Passionate about mod fashion in 1966, I was lucky enough to go the U.S. for shopping sprees, since Toronto had such limited offerings back then. I bought this outfit on a road trip my family took to visit cousins in Passaic, New Jersey.

Getting up onstage with Ronnie Hawkins for an impromptu dance at the 1969 Toronto Po
Festival was unquestionably one of my life's most exhilarating experiences.   *Photo by Norm Horne*

LEFT: Stevie Wonder was warm and wonderful when I ran into him at New York Fashion Week in 2005, excited for the presentation of his ex-wife Kai Milla's collection.

BELOW: Meeting Paul McCartney at New York's Plaza Hotel for the first time in 1984 was a total fantasy.

Beyoncé's star was rising fast when she posed for the cover of our *FQ* magazine in 2006. She suggested that her favorite photographer, Matthew Rolston, shoot this photo of us together. *Photo by Matthew Rolston*

Interviewing Keith Richards in Antigua in 1986 proved to be another fantasy realized. He was the epitome of cool.

I always felt Alexander McQueen and I shared a special bond. The conversation we had in San Francisco in 2006 was especially enlightening. The fashion world misses him madly.

In the backstage trenches with the stellar Linda Evangelista—one of the greatest models of our time— a fellow Canadian, a dear friend, and now, a fellow breast cancer survivor. *Photo by Taffi Rosen*

Paddling a canoe with the iconic Kate Moss on Rosh Hashannah was an unforgettable adventure. I was charmed by her fun spirit and down-to-earth attitude.

With the iconic Karl Lagerfeld in Versailles in 2012. Forever an inspiration, I looked at Karl as a kind of mentor. Always encouraging us to look ahead, his irreverent, quick wit always kept me on my toes.

The debonair Oscar de la Renta paid a visit to our *Fashion Television* offices back in the eighties. The warmth and wisdom he demonstrated over the years touched me deeply.

The colorful silk jacket I wore for the splashy, front-page story the late Peter Goddard wrote about me for the *Toronto Star* in 1983 marked an empowering moment in my career.

Much to my chagrin, this Canadian-designed outfit won me a spot on a magazine's worst dressed list in 1986. I quickly learned to laugh it off.

Receiving my Order of Canada medal at Ottawa's Rideau Hall in 2014 was one of my proudest moments, dressed in Lida Baday.

Covering the royal wedding of Kate and William in 2011 was another proud moment, and especially satisfying to get "the scoop."

J. D. Roberts and I were so-called video virgins when we first started hosting *The NewMusic* in 1979. We got to blaze some amazing trails.

Spending time with the brilliant Leonard Cohen in the mid eighties was the sweetest honor. He was suave and kind and I was beyond charmed.

In San Miguel de Allende on New Year's Eve 2010 with my dear friend and original style mentor, Olympian skater and artist Toller Cranston. Miss him like crazy.

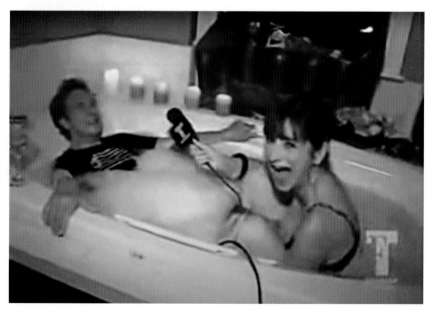

My bathtub interview with Andy Summers of The Police in 2007 was one of the most outrageous escapades—especially when his hair caught fire. *Photo Courtesy of Bell Media*

I was the picture of romantic idealism at my first wedding in 1975, in a gown I designed myself, that featured a hood rather than a veil. My daughter Joey later resurrected the gown for her music video for "Mirroring."

My daughter Bekky was such a cool little kid in the black leather moto jacket that became a style trademark for her, just as my own first black leather jacket became a staple for me growing up.

Being turned on to the beauty of the Yukon has been one of my life's great gifts, thanks to my daughter Joey, seen here wearing my seventies Suttles and Seawinds vest, with her dog Oblio.

Being inducted into Canada's Walk of Fame in 2016, with my daughters Joey and Bekky by my side, made for a heart-swelling evening. The girls both wore vintage, while I wore Greta Constantine.

Photo by George Pimentel

Meeting Iain MacInnes, the love of my life, in 2015 at the McMichael Gallery's Moonlight Gala, was a dream come true. This photo was taken the very first night we met. Talk about love at first sight!

The plaid designer coat that Iain bought me on our first trip to Scotland in 2015 symbolized so much for me.

With Iain's aunt Angela and uncle Alasdair Gillies, tasting a wee dram on an outing in the charming village of Milngavie, Scotland.

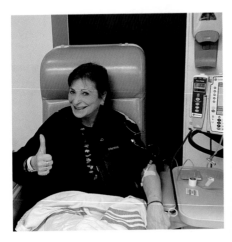

My cancer journey in 2022–23 proved to be one of the most extraordinary years of my life, and the Princess Margaret Cancer Centre became my temple of healing.

Iain's lovely aunt Angela and her delicious oaties, in her Scottish kitchen. Since she turned me on to the simple recipe, heart-shaped oaties have become a staple in my baking repertoire.

Sophisticated Lady

Little black dresses have played wonderfully supporting roles in my wardrobe, but it's the long black gowns that have always been the stars of the show. One in particular, which I sported in the early eighties, by Canadian designer Maggie Reeves, holds a special place in my heart not only for the way it made me feel but because of a memorable compliment it garnered.

My career in TV was really taking off at the start of the eighties as cohost of Citytv's *The NewMusic*. I was even more thrilled when I was offered a chance to be a general entertainment reporter for *CityPulse News*. Of course, this gig required a different wardrobe than I was used to because I'd be covering some swanky affairs. I was eager to make the investment in a few striking pieces I could rely on.

A very stylish woman by the name of Pamela Fernie, who I'd originally befriended in the midseventies, when I was living in St. John's, Newfoundland, had opened a shop right across the street from where I was living in Toronto. She was eager to dress me up for all the assignments about to come my way. After I invested in a couple of colorful silk shirts, a pair of gray gaucho pants, and a sharp gray-and-white herringbone blazer, Pam felt it was time for one more item.

"You'll get tons of use out of this dress," she said as she held up an impressive but unconventional black crepe gown.

I wasn't convinced. "I don't know, Pam," I said. "It's asymmetrical. It's a bit weird, don't you think? I mean, only one sleeve and the other arm bare? It might be a little too offbeat for me."

"Oh, nonsense! That's what makes it so striking. And the subtle bow on the one shoulder is so sweet. Not to mention the big slit up the side—it's killer! Besides, it's from the couturiere Maggie Reeves, from her new ready-to-wear collection. You've got to try it on!"

Pam was insistent, so I disappeared into the dressing room. Once I had the dress zipped up, I barely recognized myself! Who was this ultrasophisticated gal staring back at me, clad in this terribly chic, very grown-up frock? I drew back the curtain so Pam could see me.

"Oh, that is di-*vine,* darling!" she said. "See? I told you! You're ready for serious action in that gown!"

As it turns out, Pam was right. I wasn't abandoning my wardrobe of vinyl jeans, leather jackets, and microminiskirts anytime soon, but I needed to have a few more elegant pieces, too. Unfortunately, even with Pam's generous discount, the frock cost me around two hundred dollars—the highest price I'd ever paid for a piece of clothing. Still, I figured it was worth it. I left the shop feeling elated, ready for my first black-tie assignment.

A couple of weeks later, in October 1981, serious black-tie duty called. Prime Minister Pierre Elliott Trudeau was coming to town for a high-end fundraiser at the Sheraton Centre, and I was assigned to cover the party.

Relieved that I had the perfect dress to wear to this second coming of Trudeau to Toronto, I was excited to attend my first formal party assignment. And while I knew I'd never get to interview the PM, let alone get close to him, I was looking forward to wowing the guests with my seriously swish new look.

As I walked into the venue, nostalgic memories came rushing back: The last time I rode up to the ballroom on the long escalator in the lobby had been in 1975, as a young bride. How my life had changed over the course of six years! No longer married, and no longer an idealistic performing artist, I was now a single career gal, forging a path in the media. Ironically, I was dressed in dramatic black as opposed to the innocent white wedding gown I'd worn as I first rode up to that ballroom.

When I arrived I took a deep breath, and then entered the vast room. The new me was ready to schmooze. I located my cameraman, and he handed me my mic. My eyes scoured the giant scene, which was buzzing with a wide range of folks. Towards the back, I spotted the guest of honor. The dashing tuxedoed PM was sitting at a table all by himself with what looked like a security officer standing by. Did I dare approach him?

"Oh, go for it!" urged my cameraman. "The worst that can happen? He blows you off."

Easy for him to say. The thought of being rejected by Pierre Trudeau, the coolest, smartest, and classiest guy imaginable, all while wearing an unusual evening gown, was terrifying to me. But I was on a mission. How amazing would it be for me, a mere entertainment reporter, to actually get a sound bite from the country's leader?

I gathered up every ounce of courage and approached the tall gentleman who was guarding the PM.

"Excuse me. Hi, my name is Jeanne Beker, from *CityPulse News*. Is there any way I could talk to the prime minister?"

I waited for Trudeau's security guy to bite my head off, but he didn't. Instead, he said. "Hang on a minute. I'll go check."

I watched nervously as he walked over to Trudeau and leaned close to whisper in his ear. The classy PM looked over at me and my cameraman and said something to the man.

Suddenly, the man walked back towards me. "Okay," he said. "Go ahead."

"Incredible!" I said. "Thank you." And to my cameraman, I said, "Come on. Let's go!"

Before I knew it, I was leaning in towards Pierre Trudeau, microphone in hand. "Good evening, Mr. Prime Minister. So great to see you," I said.

Trudeau looked up at me. "Is that on the record, that you have lovely eyes?" he asked.

I couldn't believe he'd said that.

"Well, coming from you, that's quite a compliment, I must say," I managed to reply.

"And I like your dress, too," he said.

Score! Pam was right all along. Why had I ever doubted her? But I had no time to think about that.

"I like what you're wearing, too," I shot back.

"Oh, it's quite conventional," Trudeau demurred.

"I especially like that red rose in your lapel," I said, recovering myself. "It's so you."

That line got a chuckle out of him. He was famous for the roses in his lapel, his signature look.

I asked him a couple more questions about the event itself, but soon enough, it was time to move on and allow him some space.

Looking back on the moment now, I can't quite believe I had the chutzpah to approach the prime minister for an impromptu interview. Regardless, I'm really glad I did. To this day, I wonder how much my offbeat, dramatic black gown had to do with Trudeau allowing me a few moments of his time. Sometimes it's important to go big or go home. This is most certainly something that both Pam and Canada's revered Pierre Elliott Trudeau understood implicitly.

Big, Bold, and Beyoncé

There have been a number of precious jewelry pieces that I've especially cherished over the years, not only because of who gave them to me but because of the way they made me feel. One pair of wonderfully designed gold earrings—a gift from a dear boyfriend with great taste—hold a special place in my jewelry box. These statement earrings, consisting of intertwined bands of white and yellow gold, have always represented strength and balance to me. So in the summer of 2006, when I had the glorious chance to work with the great Beyoncé Knowles on a fall shoot for *FQ Magazine,* those were the earrings I decided to wear.

It was a hot July day, and our team had gathered at Pier59 Studios in New York, anxiously awaiting Beyoncé's arrival. On what was a very stressful press day for her, she was already over an hour late, and we were all getting antsy.

"Don't worry," said someone from her management team. "Beyoncé's so fabulous. When she gets here, it'll take no time at all."

While I'd already interviewed some of the world's biggest stars, the prospect of a cover shoot with this young powerhouse, and a solid sit-down chat with her, was a tad nerve-racking. After all, this was a major story, and our magazine was going to press in just a couple of weeks. We had to get it right. I prayed that Beyoncé would be as nice and professional as everybody said she was.

I checked myself out in the mirror at the back of the studio. I'd decided on a casual black-and-white dotted T-shirt dress, a pair of bold Elsa Peretti bangles, and my luxe-looking white and yellow gold earrings. While my frock was rather cheap and cheerful, my earrings gave me gravitas. I loved this high-low mix, which at the time was all the rage.

Suddenly, I looked to see our star making her grand entrance. She was the personification of dazzling glamour, decked out in a sequined black-and-white strapless Valentino gown and Chopard diamond earrings worth $1.6 million.

"Hi, everybody! Sorry I'm so late," she said breathlessly. "It's been nonstop today."

Beyoncé was accompanied by her own tiny creative team— stylist, makeup artist, and hairdresser. They'd prepped her to utter perfection.

"Hi, Beyoncé!" I said. "I'm Jeanne. Thank you so much for

doing this. We're all thrilled that you could fit us in. And this is our art director, Bob Makinson. . . ."

"Our magazine is oversized," explained Bob. "So we can really play with a big, dramatic image. We'll want to shoot you from head to toe."

Within minutes the creative shorthand between Beyoncé and Matthew Rolston—her photographer of choice, who'd flown in from L.A.—was established, and she expertly posed for the camera like a grand seductress. At one point, her stylist handed her a long black pair of evening gloves. She donned one and held the other over her head with both hands, arms outstretched. At twenty-five years old, this dynamo was exuding uncanny strength and confidence. As I watched, I knew we had our cover shot in the can.

"That was amazing. Thank you so much!" I said once the shoot was done. "I just can't imagine getting anything better than that."

"Well, there's another outfit we can try, just to give you an option," Beyoncé offered.

"Really? You are so generous! I know how crazy a day it was for you. . . ."

"Well, this kind of wardrobe helps me rise to any occasion," she said with a laugh. "When I feel bad, the thing that helps me throughout the day is putting on my nicest outfit and trying to look as good as I can. For whatever reason, it makes me feel better."

"Yeah, but when we're in a slump, we're not usually motivated to put that much into the way we look," I countered.

"I know. But I'm always like, 'I'm not gonna let this beat me! I'm gonna go and put on that one thing that I've been saving for a day like this.' And it kinda makes me feel like I can get through it. It just makes me feel good about myself."

Beyoncé and her style team disappeared to concoct a second look; then she came back in another drop-dead gorgeous outfit, this one a slinky gold lamé gown topped with a lush fur bolero. An electric fan blew her luscious locks off her face, and she masterfully moved in all the right ways.

After the shot she shook my art director's hand and thanked him for coming. I told her I'd see her at Sony Music Studios the next day for our in-depth interview.

"Oh, great. But let's have Matthew get a shot of us together while we've got him here."

I was overjoyed by her suggestion, and we cozied up, side by side—me in my humble dotted T-shirt dress with my luxe earrings, and Beyoncé in her swish superstar getup.

The next day, curled up on a leather couch at Sony Studios, we had a chance to get up close and personal. Beyoncé confided that while she feels fearless onstage, she grapples with self-doubt in a larger context.

"Whenever I try to do anything different, I'm scared. And if I'm not scared, then there's a problem. When you're comfortable, when you're not hungry for something and you just know that you're going to do a great job at it, then usually you don't give as much as if you were a little nervous and had to prove to yourself that you could do it."

"Well, you know what they say—the hardest thing about being a success is remaining a success . . ." I said.

"It's true. And it's tough, because I'm competing with myself.

I'm competing with the last thing I did, and I always try to be innovative and do something better and something new. And though I'm inspired by other legends, I'm always trying to do me and figure out what the next move is."

"What dreams do you have, besides just your career as a performer?"

"I want to have a family. I want to be married. Whenever it happens, my priorities will change. I mean I love and admire Madonna and the people who are able to balance both, so I don't think I'll stop singing, but I will slow down a lot. . . ."

"Hard to believe you're even entertaining thoughts about slowing down one day, when you're so in the eye of the storm now. I guess you just never really take your eye off the prize."

"I want to be around for a long time. I want people to think of quality when they think of me. I'm still figuring things out because I'm still young, and I'm still changing. But ultimately, I know who I am, and that's a comforting feeling. You can't really be confident and you can't truly fall in love and you can't truly do anything until you know what you like and what you don't and who you are. I just have to trust my gut."

All these years later, I've watched from afar as Beyoncé's success has soared to unprecedented heights. I'm convinced that her insight and self-awareness made her the incomparable superstar she is today.

The lovely portrait that Matthew Rolston took of us that magical afternoon hangs proudly in my den—a constant reminder of the power of bold style coupled with generosity of spirit and personal warmth.

Invested

It's funny the way certain garments or pieces of jewelry can reflect our past and our future at the very same time.

In 1975, when I was twenty-three, I moved to St. John's, Newfoundland, to pursue my artistry as a mime but, oddly enough, landed a job with CBC radio instead. Around the time I got my first paycheck, I fell in love with a cute little patchwork vest that I spotted in a dress shop and knew I had to have. It was designed by the Nova Scotia artisanal label Suttles and Seawinds. It's a garment I cherish to this day. And now, almost fifty years later, you might say it's a piece that's become emblematic of the special bond I share with my younger daughter, Joey.

Joey was twenty-two when she informed me that she was moving to the Yukon. A promising textile artist, she'd just been accepted to Ontario College of Art and Design University in Toronto when she heard about SOVA—Yukon School of Visual Arts—where she'd be able to do a foundation year for OCADU.

"I'll just go for a year, and then I'll be back. Don't worry, Mum. It'll be a great experience!" she said.

"But it's so incredibly far away, Jo. You don't even know anyone there," I reasoned. "Are you sure you want to go to school that far away?" I was slightly panicked at the thought of my baby flying so far from home.

"Mum, you took off for New York and Paris and Newfoundland when you were young. Why shouldn't I be able to go off on an adventure like that?" she countered.

"Well, okay," I said with a sigh. In my head, I was flashing back to my parents sending me off with their blessings when I told them I was leaving for the wilds of New York City. *As long as it's just for a year,* I thought to myself.

Then she left. And I'll never forget that day. She had her sewing machine, her guitar, and a big blue steamer trunk packed with all her favorite clothes. Joey's always had a brilliant sense of style, and on that day, she was emanating a forties movie star vibe, wearing a little vintage dress and tailored jacket. She was taking the train across Canada to Vancouver, and then a long bus ride up to the Yukon.

Her dad and I accompanied her to Union Station. My stomach was in knots as we waited for her departure. It's not that I doubted her ability to survive out there, it's that I was sending her off into the great unknown. While I was excited for her, my heart broke for myself, because I knew it was the end of an era.

My little girl wasn't little anymore. She was fully grown and independent.

"Bye, Mum," she said as I gave her a big send-off hug, while in my mind I said a little prayer.

By the end of that school year, Joey had settled really well in the Yukon, and one day she had some news. "So, Mum," she said over the phone, a bit of apprehension in her voice. "I've decided that I really don't want to study visual art anymore. I want to pursue my music."

I could deal with that. Joey was a talented singer-songwriter and guitar player. I wasn't sure I was happy about her decision to quit college, but I knew she was passionate about music, too, so that was a good thing. But I sensed she had more to say.

"I really love it here. I've fallen in love with the community. So I'd like to stay for at least another year."

My heart sank yet again. This was not what I wanted to hear. I'd thought—hoped—that Joey's romance with the Yukon would wane, and after spending a long, cold winter up there, she'd be ready to come back home in the summer. But as the ice thawed, and Joey fell more and more in love with the faraway, quirky place, she decided to dig in even deeper.

She rented a little log cabin in West Dawson, across the river from town. It was off-grid, which meant no running water, no electricity. And she was moving in there solo. Alone. In the woods. A mother's worst nightmare. I had to go out to see how she was managing.

Joey tried to prepare me before showing me her humble haven. "Just bring cozy clothes, Mum. No fancy stuff," she said.

Still, she did ask me to pull some things from her stylish closet at home: two sixties dresses and a pair of patent kitten heels. There must be the odd occasion to dress up in the Yukon? Gazing at her trove of vintage clothing—a finely edited collection of well-worn dresses from bygone days culled from Toronto's funkiest shops—brought tears to my eyes. I remembered her coming home with each precious garment—a treasured find she'd lovingly style, hair done up in pin curls, her figure rocking frocks the way they were meant to be worn. I'd drink in every ounce of her—the gorgeous young woman she'd become, with an amazing style sense all her own, light-years from the high-fashion labels some girls her age craved.

"This one's a true original," I said to myself, proud that Joey had her own unique way of seeing the world.

Two plane rides, an overnight in Whitehorse, and another small plane ride later, I arrived in Dawson City. I didn't have to do much more than walk around town with Joey (a feat easily accomplished since there are merely a handful of streets in Dawson, and only one main drag) to understand why she'd embraced this community.

People of all ages greeted us warmly, and Joey eagerly introduced me as her mum. Some people recognized me as "that woman from *Fashion Television*," but what was far sweeter was being the mum of one of the Klondike's newest community members. I thought I'd burst with pride the first time one of the resident artists thanked me for "sharing Joey with Dawson City."

"She's added so much to the community," the woman enthused.

"She's such a great musician, and she's been teaching the kids ukulele and got involved with the play they staged. She's inspiring. We love having her here," she said.

My feelings of comfort quickly dissolved, though, when we took the ferry across the mighty Yukon River to visit Joey's tiny cabin. Buried in the backwoods, down a mucky trail, the two-room log abode was cozy, all right, but it boasted only limited, solar-powered electricity and a classic outhouse out the back. There was no running water and only a small woodstove for warmth. I wondered how she planned on coping with that fifty-seven-degrees-below-zero temperature she'd braved the past winter in town. But I didn't dare ask for fear she'd think I was challenging her.

Evidently, my silence spoke volumes.

"Don't you like it?" Joey asked in earnest, dismayed that I wasn't jumping for joy about her new digs. How could my child give up the luxury of our beautiful, big city home for the spartan likes of this godforsaken rustic cabin?

Sensing I couldn't answer her question, Joey said, "I'm just going to change, Mum, before we head back out to town for dinner." Then she disappeared into her wee bedroom.

Two minutes later, out waltzed Joey, and my heart just about melted. There was my gorgeous girl, sun streaming through the cabin window, looking like some kind of angelic apparition. And she was wearing my old Suttles and Seawinds patchwork vest! I'd given it to her a few years back when she was on the hunt for seventies fare. Suddenly, there was a little bit of Newfoundland in the room, a little bit of the younger, more impetuous me. I was reminded of my own idealism and the adventurous dreams I'd entertained when I was Joey's age.

"What?" Joey asked. "Why are you looking at me that way?"

"Because you look great," I said.

It had taken me a moment to adjust to everything, but I saw it clearly now—my brave, gorgeous daughter and how happy she was with her new life, living in nature, writing her beautiful music, and truly blazing her own, adventurous trails.

Everything had come full circle. And all was right with the world.

Rebel Spirit

If there's one garment that's totally emblematic of a rebel spirit, it's a black leather moto jacket. Just try one on and you immediately feel supercool—tough, kinda chic, and ultimately invincible. I got my first black leather jacket, though not exactly a biker style, at the age of fourteen, from our next-door neighbor, Tibor Berk. He was a traveling coat salesman who had some leftover samples in his station wagon. He'd evidently decided his own fourteen-year-old daughter wasn't the "black leather jacket" type, but somehow, he thought I might be just right for the garment, despite my parents' trepidation, of course!

I was thrilled with Mr. Berk's cool and generous castoff, a piece that injected new edge and gravitas into my trendy teenage wardrobe, marking me as an independent thinker and fearless trailblazer (or so I thought). Twenty years later, I was given a tiny black moto jacket for my firstborn, Bekky, by the Canadian leather design company Danier. The label had been sponsoring my wardrobe for *Fashion Television* in the late eighties and generously offered me the ultimate in cool kids' wear. I was delighted, and so was the precocious Bekky, who was about five years old when she grew into her glorious little fashion statement.

I'm not sure if Bekky instinctively knew that her black leather moto jacket made her look irresistibly cute to all grown-ups. And I wonder if she realized that it also gave her power on the playground. Always fussy about what she wore to kindergarten, Bekky put up a fight about what she wanted—and didn't want—to wear. But I can't remember hearing any arguments about the wee biker jacket. Evidently, it was a piece she felt totally comfortable in, and because she wore it so often, it became part of her signature five-year-old style, and something she wore for a good couple of years after that.

As time passed, Bekky became a savvy and confident youngster. She was also whipsmart and never afraid to speak her mind. I remember being in her younger sister, Joey's, bedroom with her at bedtime one night shortly after their dad had moved out. Bekky was ten and Joey was eight, and I ached with sadness for them both. They loved their dad so much—as did I. There had never been any arguing in our house, so neither of my kids was quite clear on why this was happening. Joey was especially distraught.

"Why doesn't Dad want to live with us, Mummy?" she asked between sobs. "Doesn't he love us?"

"Yes, of course he loves you guys—very, very much," I told her.

"Joey, don't you get it?" Bekky said. "Dad just isn't happy here."

"Darlings, like I said, your dad loves you both, but he doesn't love *me* the same way anymore. That's why he's moved out," I explained.

"Oh, Mummy, that's not true," Joey insisted. "I know Daddy loves you, too!"

"Joey!" Bekky said, even more firmly this time. "Get it through your head. Dad isn't in love with Mum anymore."

At the age of ten, Bekky was mature enough to accept this cold, hard fact, as heartbreaking and devastating as it was to me, her sister, and to her. That's just the way it is with Bekky—she's always been so direct and clear about her emotions.

The years that followed, raising my two young beauties as a single, working mum, weren't easy. They saw their dad every Wednesday evening and every other weekend. But I was on my own much of the time, mastering a balancing act of the highest order, trying to be there for my kids while keeping up with this monstrously intense career I'd created for myself. And Bekky, my bright and beautiful, wild-spirited older daughter, was forever challenging me, as most mothers of teenage girls can understand all too well.

One thing I was never prepared to fight over was the subject of style. When my daughters were young, there was no stopping them if they wanted to wear tutus to school, mix outrageous colors, go around with pant legs dragging on the floor, or wear ripped garments held together with safety pins. I decided to bite my tongue rather than impose any notions of style propriety on my girls. Each of them had a strong sense of who she was and was entitled to express herself as long as she wasn't hurting anyone.

Bekky was especially bohemian in her fashion approach and mixed things in unexpected and unconventional ways. She would wear hot pants with sheer hose in subzero temperatures. And when she was in grade eight, she boldly dyed her hair fuchsia. I cringed when she paired a tattered vintage dress with my precious gold Manolo Blahnik strappy heels and ended up running through a muddy field the rainy night of her prom, delivering the shoes back to me in less than pristine condition. *Did it matter?* I asked myself. Not so much—they were only shoes, after all.

I bit my tongue over Bekky's first belly-button piercing—yet another act of rebellion. And when her first small tattoo followed soon after, I knew I had to accept it. Then came another—a subtle nod to my own romantic past, with a quote inspired by my favorite William Blake poem emblazoned on her wrist: "To see a world in a grain of sand . . ." The next tattoo she got was of a big bee. I'd once jokingly mentioned that if I were ever to get a tattoo, it would be of a bee, for Beker, just behind my knee. Of course, I had a teensy, comical insect in mind, while Bekky's gargantuan, detailed bee was something out of a Victorian cabinet of curiosities. Still, after some time spent adjusting, I learned to love that tattoo.

In the end, I think my laissez-faire approach to Bekky's choices meant many fewer fights between us. And I think the respect I showed both girls as they finessed their own senses of style wasn't only appreciated but also reciprocated.

These days I marvel each time Bekky expresses herself. Her original fashion sense and unique voice continue to evolve in wonderful ways. In 2015 Bekky asked me if she and her partner could move to our family farm full-time. Basically, she wanted to adopt the country lifestyle I so adored but could only afford to live part-time. My heart pretty much burst with joy. It was as though she really understood and appreciated what I ultimately prioritized. Happily, her request came at a time when I'd just fallen in love with Iain, and my fantasies about running off into the sunset with him abounded. I was hardly using the farm property, so why not let Bekky move in?

"And we'd like to start an animation studio at the farm," Bekky explained. They had both earned degrees in animation and couldn't wait to open up shop. "We'd also like to start farming some of the land ourselves," she said.

"Sounds amazing," I told her.

True to form, Bekky has proved to be such an original, and she's still blazing her own trails, having produced award-winning animated films and music videos, teaching experimental animation, and savoring farm life.

I'm so proud and happy that she has found her calling and her path, and I'm pleased, too, that I could help her realize a few of her dreams.

I often think back to that feisty little firecracker of a girl in her tiny black leather moto jacket, digging her heels in, often frustrating me with her defiance, yet always impressing me with her tenacity and boundless imagination. Somehow, that young rebel turned into a daughter who is often my rock and solid foundation. To this day, she helps me see parts of myself, and the world, in brave and wondrous ways.

Class Act

I've been lucky enough to have had countless conversations with iconic figures in the design industry, philosophizing about the art and craft of fashion. That being said, it's when these famous people philosophize about life that I'm really moved, because those conversations give me insight into what drives them.

Oscar de la Renta was undeniably one of American fashion's classiest and most charming designers. Born in the Dominican Republic, Oscar left for Spain when he was only eighteen. He soon began apprenticing with the great Cristóbal Balenciaga and later moved to Paris, where he worked as a couture assistant at the house of Lanvin before taking off for New York in the early sixties to work for Elizabeth Arden. He started his own eponymous label in 1965, and the rest is American fashion history.

I interviewed Oscar countless times over the years and always felt a special bond with him. Perhaps it was because he was the only major international designer who actually came to our *Fashion Television* offices back in 1987 on a visit to Toronto. Perhaps it's also because he gave me a lovely print cocktail dress years ago, a dress I cherish to this day. It will always hold a special place in my wardrobe—and my heart.

Oscar worked for the French house of Balmain, where he designed from 1992 to 2002. His show was the first Parisian haute couture show I ever covered for *Fashion Television*. (In the earlier years of our show, I was sent to Paris only to cover the prêt-à-porter shows.)

I was overwhelmed with excitement and undeniably a little nervous about attending the intimate, high-class showing, held at the swank InterContinental Hotel in 1993. Dazzled by the exquisitely elegant offerings that were sent out that morning, I was intimidated to make my way backstage postshow for the sound bites I needed from the legend himself. But the moment I met the suave and affable Oscar, a feeling of comfort and calm swept over me.

"Hello, angel," he said by way of greeting. "Thank you for coming. I hope you liked the show."

I was tickled to be greeted so warmly. Though I knew Oscar called a lot of people "angel," somehow he made each one of us feel special by doing so.

"That show was just amazing," I gushed. "So very beautiful. You certainly are a master."

"So glad you appreciated it," he replied, "but I really have to give credit to the ateliers in Paris. These talented artisans are such a joy to work with, and they play such an important part in making the magic. Of course I love working on my own collections in New York, but creating couture in Paris really is a major fantasy for me. . . . Hope to see you next month at New York Fashion Week, angel," he said as we air-kissed goodbye.

I had many chances to converse with Oscar over the years—but there was something especially memorable about the time I was conscripted by the Hudson's Bay Company to host their in-store launch of his fragrance Live in Love. At this point, age seventy-nine, Oscar's health was failing—he'd been fighting brain cancer—but he was as suave, charming, and generous as ever.

"We have to make sure that we can find a dress for Jeanne to wear," he told his right-hand person, who'd accompanied him on the trip. We were sitting in the lounge of The Room, the swish designer section of The Bay, waiting for our public appearance. Within minutes a Bay staffer arrived with the most divine little black-and-gold silk cocktail frock, featuring a delicate feather print motif.

"Yes, if that's her size, it's wonderful!" said Oscar. "Go try it on, angel. Hope it fits."

Minutes later I was strutting the lovely dress for Oscar's approval.

"What do you think?" I asked.

"Ah, looks great on you, angel," he replied.

While Oscar seemed a little more tired and a tad more fragile than I'd ever seen him before, the twinkle in his eye was still there and the warmth he exuded was as authentic as ever.

There are few sartorial joys that can compare with the feeling of modeling a luxurious creation concocted by the person sitting right in front of you. But as I interviewed Oscar, I knew he was as happy with how I looked in his dress as I was about interviewing him in front of a crowd.

"The name alone of your new fragrance, Live in Love, is such a beautiful sentiment, and really speaks of your whole passion for living," I said as the crowd watched. "Why did you feel this was the spirit that you wanted to evoke?"

"Well, obviously the most important part of the fragrance is the juice itself, but then you want to put that into a beautiful bottle, and you want to have a great name for it, because the name has a message of what you want that fragrance to be," he said.

Oscar went on to explain where he got the idea for the name. An Italian man he'd been working with very closely for a few years, who ran all his sample rooms, was helping him come up with names. That's when Oscar noticed the tattoo on the man's arm—"Live in Love."

"I thought, *My goodness! Why didn't anyone ever think of calling a fragrance Live in Love before?* After all, it's the way we all so strongly aspire to live life—loving what surrounds you, loving your life, loving what you've made of your life, loving the moment, loving the time . . ."

I was impressed by his answer and his willingness to get to the root of some deeper emotions. I decided to launch into what I really wanted people to hear about—and perhaps what I needed to hear myself.

"We're living in an age in which the older we get, the more

productive we can become if we choose to. And you're an example of that," I told him.

"I sound like an old record, but the other day I was talking to my doctor about a friend of ours who retired, and the way his life has changed so much. And my doctor said something to me that I keep repeating every single day. He said, 'When you rest, you rust.'"

"That's going to be my new mantra!" I told the crowd.

"And it's true," said Oscar.

"I guess we just have to pray to the powers-that-be every day that we have the strength and energy to keep on going. It's not always easy," I said.

"You know, I'm doing today far much better work than I did twenty, thirty, forty years ago—for the very simple reason that I know more. I have seen more, I have learned more, I have observed more. There's a whole wealth of knowledge that I have today that I did not have when I originally started. And especially today, there is so much access to quick learning that didn't exist back then," Oscar said.

He went on to talk about his work and what torture it is to actually create a collection, despite all his passion. "There's so much doubt that's part of the creative process," he confided. "It's like a nightmare. You have to prove yourself every time."

"But the fact that you want to subject yourself to all that is what I find so miraculous and wonderful," I noted.

"But that is the curiosity of life," he replied. "I always say that the day I say I know it all, that day I should stop."

Our time was drawing to an end. "Thank you so much for

coming to Toronto, Oscar, and for creating this beautiful new scent," I said, wrapping up. But Oscar wasn't ready to wrap just yet.

"You know, the other day I was having a horrible time with someone, and I came to the conclusion that actually the biggest luxury in life has nothing to do with money and wealth. The biggest luxury in life is to be able to say what you want to say, when you want to say it. And I want to say how happy I am to know you, because it's been . . . well, we don't want to say how many years! But I knew that I was coming to Toronto and that I was going to see you. And that made me happy. And at the end, that is what life is all about."

That was my last interview with Oscar. And those were his parting words to me.

Three years later, on October 20, 2014, at the age of eighty-two, Oscar passed away from complications of cancer, the disease he'd been living with for eight years.

Serendipitously, I say this because I'm sure the angels were involved, I was at a Toronto vintage boutique trying on dresses for an upcoming event when I got a call with the news. The dress I had on was a bright red Oscar de la Renta gown.

After ending the call, I bought the dress immediately. And that dress, together with the Oscar de la Renta cocktail frock I wore for my last interview with him—a frock he gave me after the interview—are among my most treasured designer label dresses.

I've learned a lot in fashion's trenches, but few designers have imparted more to me about life than the debonair and philosophical Oscar.

Guiding Star

The seeds for so much of what I've accomplished in my life were planted by my brilliant sister, Marilyn. She's the kind of big sister who always helped illuminate my path when we were growing up, who turned me on to all things cool—from Chinese fairy tales to beatniks and Bob Dylan. Marilyn is forever encouraging me to dream big.

From a very young age, my sister aspired to be a writer, and when she actually landed a gig as an entertainment reporter for a major Toronto newspaper at the age of twenty-one—the youngest writer ever to receive a byline there—she showed me that dreams really do come true.

My own dream at the time was to become an actress, and Marilyn never seemed to doubt that I had true star potential. For my sixteenth birthday, she gave me a most precious gift: a small pin in the shape of a star, custom-made by a local silversmith. It was a simple, elegant, and powerful talisman that was unequivocally emblematic of how very much she believed in me.

"Oh, it is so beautiful!" I exclaimed when I opened the tiny box the pin was nestled in.

"I had it made especially for you," Marilyn said.

"I absolutely love it. I'm going to wear it everywhere!"

"You really are gonna make it someday. Just never take no for an answer. We deserve to be rich and famous!" she said with a laugh.

I had no idea of all the pitfalls of showbiz at the time. But Marilyn was adamant about applauding the stars in my eyes, and she gave me her blessing. Meanwhile, my parents were far from thrilled when they heard me talking about wanting to be an actress.

"Those movie stars have such terrible marriages," my mother warned. "They're all so unhappy. Show business is a dangerous business."

I knew my mum just wanted to protect me, but I was determined to go for it regardless. I wasn't sure how to make my dream happen, but I figured if I kept my focus, opportunities would knock. And so they did. . . .

Just a couple of months after my sixteenth birthday, my friend Marsha found out about an open casting call at the CBC for a new sitcom called *Toby*. Initially, I was reluctant to go downtown to this intimidating open audition. After all, I had no professional acting experience—only a series of drama lessons and a few starring roles in summer camp plays. But with Marsha's coaxing, I took my chances. With my long hair done up in two high ponytails, I donned my new hot-pink, two-piece knit outfit, complete with a flirty pleated miniskirt, then added a pair of go-go boots and my precious silver star pin. I looked in the mirror, pleased with the look I'd created.

On the long bus ride down to the CBC building on Jarvis Street, I nervously toyed with my little star pin, fluctuating between feelings of self-doubt and the responsibility I felt to myself and my sister to try my best. Marilyn believed I could do it. If she believed in me, shouldn't I believe in myself?

When I arrived, I was directed to a huge room filled with dozens of hopefuls, all of them clutching beefy résumés and glossy headshots. I didn't have anything like that, but I did have chutzpah—that, and my star pin.

I did the audition, and magically, I was cast in a recurring role in the series. I got my actors' union card and an agent and was soon going to all kinds of auditions, even landing a few roles in TV commercials. I also got some film work and landed a supporting role in *Class of '44,* the sequel to the hit movie *Summer of '42.* And I scored a starring role in an episode of the syndicated dramatic TV series *Dr. Simon Locke,* which aired on NBC. I took off to New York to study acting at nineteen, but after a year, I decided to further my academic education and came back to Toronto to study theater at York University. It was then that I became obsessed with learning an exacting technique and got intrigued with the art of mime.

In 1973, as I've said, I went to Paris to study mime with a master. While I was in love with the City of Light, I lived in a tiny hotel room and, despite my inspiring mime classes, wrestled with bouts of extreme loneliness. Meanwhile, my sister had taken a hiatus from her successful writing career and was living on a yoga retreat in northern Michigan, learning about life from a brilliant yoga master named J. Oliver Black, a disciple of Paramahansa Yogananda, who first introduced yoga to the Western world back in the 1950s. She sent me lengthy letters filled with words of hope and encouragement. Her spiritual strength and wisdom helped see me through those tough times.

"The reason I came to yoga," Marilyn wrote, "the reason I meditate, is that when you come to know your real self, you will always have this friend, this companion, this perfect, wise teacher to guide and cheer you. That teacher is really your higher self. Some call it God. But it means yourself after all. So look within, because in all the world, there is no one like you."

Again, twenty-five years later, when my marriage abruptly ended in 1998 and I was in a very dark place, my sister, now living in Los Angeles, helped bring me back from the brink.

"Remember who you are," she wrote in one of her letters. I really took that to heart. And somehow, it helped.

Though Marilyn and I have lived thousands of miles apart, she's always had a strong presence in my life, and I continue to be inspired by the trails she blazes for herself while still managing to blaze others for me. Most recently she decided to leave California after forty years of living there and move back to northern Michigan. That's where she had met her wonderful husband, Greg, back in the seventies, and they'd purchased some land there decades ago with the intention of building a home when they retired. Recently, they both boldly and bravely gave up their jobs, sold their house in L.A., packed up all their stuff, and took off to live their woodland dream.

While most people Marilyn's age are content to simply retire and relax, my vibrant and intrepid big sister keeps pushing herself to follow new dreams. To this day, she continues to be my guiding star. And happily, I still have her shining pin to remind me of all the light she's always cast my way.

Feel It All Over

As visually arresting and inspiring as fashion can be, ultimately, it's the feeling of a garment—the sensation of it against one's body and how it buoys the spirit—that we remember most. When it comes to utter flamboyance, there are few garments in my sentimental stash that can compare with the full-length tan shearling coat with a leopard-print motif stamped on the lining. Large and luxurious with a fluffy collar, this coat is all about sensual exuberance. It was designed by Canadian outerwear designer Domenic Bellissimo, who generously presented it to me in the fall of 2004 in the hope that I'd strut it on TV and garner some attention for his label.

When the New York Fashion Week shows for fall rolled out in February 2005, I could think of no better overcoat to keep me warm and looking great while running from show to show. Celebrity sightings at all the usual shows were commonplace, with some star appearances even becoming a little predictable. So there was always excitement in the air when a new label appeared on the schedule. After all, you never knew what celebrities might come out to support their designer pals.

While we hadn't heard much about the new Kai Milla label that was set to make its debut at the show, the fashion press did know one thing for sure: Stevie Wonder would be in attendance. The Motown legend was married to the label's designer, Kai Millard, a former freelance art director he'd met in 1999. They had a child together—a boy named Kailand—with another on the way. There was little doubt that Stevie himself would be attending Kai's first big show to lend his support, and my cameraman and I were psyched about the opportunity to catch up with him and his wife.

I'd interviewed Stevie years before for *The NewMusic* and was charmed by his cool, gentle nature and great sense of humor. His music held a special place in my heart. The morning after my daughter Bekky was born, her father, who hosted a morning radio show, played "Isn't She Lovely" as a dedication to me and our new baby. I'd always been a big Stevie fan, and the chance to see him in the context of a fashion show was particularly intriguing. I wondered how the legendary blind musician might digest the impending spectacle. How would he take it in, and what would it mean to him to experience his wife's work on display?

We got to the show early. A few people had just begun to filter in, and suddenly, there in the front row, I spotted Stevie. I made a beeline for him, my cameraman in tow.

"Hi, Stevie!" I said warmly. "It's Jeanne Beker—I used to be a music journalist and interviewed you in Toronto a while back for the Canadian show *The NewMusic*. But I'm covering the fashion scene now."

"Hey, Jeanne! Great that you could come today," he replied. "Guess we're all getting into fashion these days." He laughed then, and so did I.

"We're very excited to see your wife's collection."

"Oh, it's good. Real good. Can't wait to hear what you think of it." I could tell Stevie was very proud of Kai.

"Stevie, I've got my cameraman here. Do you mind if we get a sound bite from you?"

"Okay, that's cool."

My cameraman started rolling and I began to quiz Stevie about Kai's work and his feelings about fashion in general.

"You know, I've designed some of my own costumes," he told me. "For me, it's got to be about comfort. And I work with people who describe the prints and colors to me, because I know clothes can express so much to your audience. . . . Fashion is so important for any performer. I really do love it."

"But what about the clothes that Kai's designing?" I asked. "How are you perceiving them?"

"Oh, they're so beautiful. I can feel the textures of the fabrics, and I can hear the rustle of the clothing. . . . I just know these clothes are very sensual and very feminine and very sexy."

I thanked Stevie for the sound bite and told him we'd catch up with him backstage afterwards. I took off my coat, took my seat in the crowd, and got ready for the show.

Kai's collection was elegant, sensual, and sumptuous, just as Stevie had intimated. At the end of the presentation, the pregnant designer was joined at the top of the runway by their young son, Kailand, decked out in a little navy blue velvet suit. Stevie got up from his seat to join his family onstage. It was a lovely family moment.

Later Stevie was talking to a scrum of reporters. He was glowing, thrilled to be there, and so proud of his wife. But evidently he was also aware of the fact that not many understood how someone who was visually impaired could interpret fashion design. From my position in the scrum, I called out a question, asking him how he processed Kai's work and what about it gave him the greatest satisfaction.

"The whole idea of Kai and her design is that it has the essence of love and clothing," he said.

Stevie was adamant about singing the lovely Kai's praises, and I was totally charmed by the obvious love and respect he had for her and her new initiative. He went on to comment about texture, how he's always loved the feeling of fabrics, especially silk and velvet.

"Some textures I've never even known before," he said. "It's a great discovery for me . . . how art and design and a love for it all comes together to create beautiful things."

I'd never heard fashion described quite this way before, through the sense of touch, and I found his words so meaningful.

As we left for the next show on our schedule, I stepped out into the freezing February afternoon, wrapped in my long shearling coat. I took Stevie's words to heart, and as if for the first time, I really felt the softness of the leather I was wearing, the smooth warmth of the lining against my skin. That coat was luxury and coziness all in one perfect garment.

I still have a precious photo that was snapped of me in that wild, statement-making coat, sitting next to Stevie in the front row of Kai's show. It rests in a frame on my piano—a constant reminder of the importance of "feel" when it comes to fashion, music, and great art in general.

O Canada!

There's one thing that inspires me to put my right hand over my heart every single day: It's a tiny silver-and-white enamel pin, shaped like a snowflake, with a maple leaf in its center. I wear this pin almost every day, whether I'm in an evening gown or a tracksuit, and it's among my most treasured pieces of jewelry. It's a revered privilege to sport this little pin as it signifies my induction into the highest level of distinction in the Canadian honors system.

I was named to the Order of Canada in December 2013. Of all the honors bestowed on me over the course of my career, being recognized in this way has given me the ultimate satisfaction. Of course, I never dreamed that any of my accomplishments would lead to that heart-exploding moment when I proudly stood in

Ottawa's Rideau Hall and the Queen's representative, Governor General David Johnston, presented me with a gleaming grand medal. The little pin, which had been sent to my home a few months beforehand, had already become my very best accessory.

There was no question that my older daughter, Bekky, would be by my side for the ceremony in Ottawa in 2014, though sadly, my younger daughter, Joey, was living in the Yukon, and my mum wasn't well enough to make the trip. Bekky and I then got a priceless invitation we couldn't refuse from Laureen Harper, Prime Minister Stephen Harper's charming and ebullient wife, whom I had met six years earlier. That time Laureen had heard, through a mutual friend, that my mum and I would be visiting Ottawa for a Holocaust memorial. And since Laureen had been a fan of *Fashion Television,* she wanted to meet me. So she extended a very gracious invitation to us to come to 24 Sussex Drive for dinner.

When my mother and I visited their home that first time, Mum could not have been happier about dining with the wife of the prime minister. We all hit it off wonderfully, and a strong friendship formed between Laureen and me. In the years that followed, we shared several fun adventures together. When I told her I was coming to Ottawa for the Order of Canada induction, she insisted that Bekky and I spend the night before the ceremony at her residence.

"It'll be totally convenient for you," Laureen enthused over the phone. "Rideau Hall, where the ceremony and dinner are taking place, is right across the road from us!"

"Well, twist my arm!" I said, buoyed by the generous offer. "It'll be quite the experience for Bekky." Even as I said it, I was not quite sure how my very left-of-center artist daughter would react to being in the Conservative PM's pad. Nonetheless, I couldn't wait for her to meet the lovely Laureen.

As expected, Bekky was totally charmed by the prime minister's wife. Laureen's passion for animal welfare knew no bounds, and we were delighted by the big attic room that was filled with a host of tiny kittens Laureen was fostering. Bekky and I spent that night in the third-floor guest room. It was like something out of a fairy tale. I'd never felt so grateful and so secure. And no wonder! RCMP officers were stationed outside the house. After all, this was the residence of the leader of our country. All night I kept wondering: *How did I, the child of Holocaust survivors who had lost everything in the war, end up staying the night at the home of Canada's prime minister?*

When morning came, I persuaded Bekky to come down to the kitchen in her pj's. "Laureen is so wonderfully unpretentious! You don't have to get dressed for breakfast," I said.

"Okay, Mum, but if Stephen Harper is down there, don't leave me alone with him!" she replied. "I can't imagine what we'd talk about."

"Oh, Bekky, this family is very cool, I assure you. Don't even worry about it."

As we made our way to the kitchen, we passed the large foyer, where Stephen was sitting in a chair getting his hair cut. We nodded and continued on. In the kitchen, Laureen sat casually at the table with Charlie, her beloved pet rescue chinchilla, on her lap.

"Good morning!" she called out, then proceeded to tell us how Charlie loved eating the little pieces of dried fruit that came with the boxed cereal that was on the table. To our delight, we watched Laureen feed Charlie bits of berries as though a pet chinchilla at the prime minister's kitchen table was the most natural thing ever.

A few minutes later, Stephen entered. "Okay, she's ready for you!" he said, referring to the hairstylist in the foyer. Laureen had booked stylist appointments not only for her husband but also for me on my big day.

I quickly introduced the PM to Bekky, and they exchanged pleasantries.

"Will you excuse me?" Laureen said and left the room with Charlie.

"See you in a few minutes," I said to Bekky. "I have to go get my hair styled." As I was leaving, Stephen sat down at the breakfast table with my daughter.

I made my way toward the foyer inwardly cringing about leaving my spirited, pj-wearing daughter alone with the prime minister in his kitchen. What would happen? Would she ask him pressing questions? Would they get into a heated political argument?

I had my hair styled, a little bit anxious the whole time. But when I got back to the kitchen, my daughter and Stephen were all smiles. As it turned out, they got along famously. The prime minister soon excused himself, and Bekky and I were alone.

"What did you talk about?" I excitedly asked her.

"Oh, nothing much, really," she said matter-of-factly. "He asked me about what I did, and I told him I was studying in Montreal. Then he advised me to invest in real estate."

It was certainly a great suggestion, and though she was in no position to act on the advice, it was the kind of sage, fatherly guidance my dad had always given me.

"Is that it? Is that all you talked about?" I prodded.

"What did you think would happen, Mum? Did you think I'd launch into a leftist diatribe?"

Evidently my fears were unfounded. As usual, Bekky held her own—pj's and all. And I was crazy proud of her for all her aplomb in what must have been a surreal and unnerving encounter for her.

Later that day at the Order of Canada ceremony, I received the biggest honor of my life. I consider my Order of Canada pin my very best accessory. It reminds me to never rest on my laurels and to constantly strive to do better. It also serves as a memento of what this country is ideally all about for me—love, generosity, acceptance, inclusion, and maintaining a sense of humor—especially when you're dealing with opinionated daughters and berry-loving chinchillas at the breakfast table.

Lost and Found

Of all the signature accessories I ever held dear in my life, I always felt my silver Elsa Peretti wrist cuff was the most impressive. The beautifully designed piece, created by the late talented Spanish jewelry designer in the seventies, was inspired by Antoni Gaudí's Casa Milà in Barcelona. The cuff has an organic, fluid form, molded in the shape of a wrist, and I wore mine proudly almost every day, for twenty-five years.

The exquisite bracelet was given to me by my ex-boyfriend Jack—who swept me off my feet after my second marriage broke up in 1998. Jack was a dashing and generous fellow—the son of a dear old family friend, and I'd known him my whole life. It was as though Jack resuscitated me after my husband left. He helped me feel human again. Our first Chanukah together, I was in bed, just waking up, when Jack walked into the room and presented me with an iconic turquoise box.

"Oh my god! A gift from *Tiffany's*?" I squealed. "I've never received a gift from Tiffany's before. The box alone is so beautiful, I don't even want to open it!" Still, I gleefully clutched that gorgeous box.

"Just open it!" Jack said with a laugh.

I could tell he was very excited to see my reaction to this, his very first gift to me. There was no question that whatever he'd chosen, he'd done so with great care. Jack was very thoughtful and had exquisite taste. I knew even before opening the box that this was something that would have great sentimental meaning to me.

I sat up in bed and removed the box's white satin ribbon. I opened the lid and gasped. Inside was the gleaming silver cuff, an *objet d'art* worthy of Wonder Woman! I immediately slipped it on my wrist and started weeping.

"So I guess you like it?" asked Jack.

"Like it? I adore it! Thank you soooo much. This is the most amazing present you could have given me. I'll cherish it always."

Not only was the cuff incredibly stylish, it was also very empowering. From the moment I put it on, I felt a surge of confidence, as though I was finally healing from all the heartbreak I'd endured. I knew it would be part of my everyday wardrobe from then on, a monumental touchstone that would constantly remind me that I was lovable and strong, and that a whole new life awaited me.

Though some fashion trends change, that silver cuff remained a constant for over two decades. Whenever I wanted a pop of power or a touch of class, which was most days, I'd slip it onto my wrist.

I celebrated my seventieth birthday in March 2022 convinced that I was infallible. My career was still rolling along, and there were new projects on the horizon. My daughters were both in good places; I'd settled down with Iain, the love of my life; and my health seemed top notch. I faced the new decade with power and excitement. And then, just a couple of months after my big birthday celebration, I got a daunting call. I'd gone for my routine mammogram and was informed they'd found "a mass"—a tumor that measured almost three centimeters. I was asked to come back to the hospital for a biopsy and an ultrasound. Something wasn't right. I was scared stiff.

I spent the next few days in a very dark place, imagining the worst, googling late into the night, going down untold rabbit holes while trying so hard to remain hopeful. Maybe it was nothing—just a cyst or a benign tumor? Surely that happened all the time. But while I underwent the breast ultrasound and was being poked and prodded for my biopsy, the attending doctor suggested I get an MRI as well. I knew what this meant—she didn't like what she saw.

A couple of days later, I had my MRI. And then another couple of days later, just as Iain and I were about to launch into a plate of wings at our favorite country pub, my phone's caller ID lit up with my doctor's name.

"Jeanne, where are you?" my doctor asked. "I have the results of your biopsy and MRI. And I'm afraid it's bad news. Would you like to come to my office to discuss, or . . . ?"

"Just give it to me, Dr. Curtis," I said, resigned to the life-altering news I was about to receive.

The doctor told me I'd been diagnosed with HER2 triple-positive breast cancer—not exactly the worst kind you can get, but not the best either—if there is ever such a thing. It looked like they'd caught it early, though, which was the best news of all, and there didn't appear to be any lymph node involvement, but we couldn't be sure until I had surgery. Dr. Curtis was going to refer me to the best surgeon she knew at Toronto's mighty Princess Margaret Cancer Centre.

"But do you think I'll be okay, Dr. Curtis?" I asked with trepidation.

"You'll go through a journey. But . . . you'll be okay," she reassured me. I couldn't be certain Dr. Curtis was right—nor likely could she. But her words provided comfort when I needed it most.

For the next week or two, before I got to meet my oncological surgeon, I was in a precarious place, constantly jumping between fear and faith. I wore my "Wonder Woman" silver cuff constantly to help me remember my resilience. I was indeed a survivor, with the personal power to overcome just about anything.

I walked through the doors of Princess Margaret Hospital on May 31, 2022, feeling a mix of confidence and apprehension. This was one place I never wanted to go. I remembered my mum talking about he Princess Margaret Hospital—which was founded as the Ontario Cancer Institute in 1952, the year I was born. Whenever we drove past, my mum would recall how she'd lost several friends to cancer. "Oy, that's such a good hospital, but

Got zol offheeten (which is Yiddish for "God forbid"), you never want to be there," she'd say. "Just pray that we never need it."

It's funny how some sayings or phrases can really make a difference when you're facing news like I was. For some reason, I had a quote attributed to Confucius playing over and over again in my mind: "Wherever you go, go with all your heart." I kept repeating that to myself as I rode the elevator to the second-floor Breast Clinic. And somehow, as I stepped out of the elevator, I perceived this initially daunting and unfamiliar new environment as a temple of healing: This is where I was going to get the support I needed to make it through the darkness that had descended on my life.

Dr. Tulin Cil is someone who radiates light and banishes darkness. From the moment I met her, I felt better about my situation. She reiterated that, thankfully, my cancer was caught early, and I'd have a couple of options for treatment—either surgery first, then chemo and radiation, or the reverse. Dr. Cil was an oncological surgeon, but I'd have to meet with the oncologist, Dr. Eitan Amir, who would help me decide which route to take.

"You mean I'm going to be okay, Dr. Cil?" I asked.

"Yes," she reassured me. "You're going to be okay."

"Oh thank God!" I said, the tears springing to my eyes.

"What did you think I was going to say?" she asked with a smile.

"I thought I might be told that I had six months left!" I said, knowing just how much I'd struggled to keep positive in the days leading up to my appointment.

Another week went by, and I met the brilliant Dr. Amir, a

rock star figure who coolly and compassionately presented me with my options.

"So it's treatable?" I asked him once he'd run through everything.

"It's not only treatable, it's curable," he replied.

A miracle drug called Herceptin, which was approved for use in Canada in 2000, was going to be a big factor in keeping my cancer at bay. I'd start taking it intravenously the day of my first chemo treatment, which would take me through the summer, and subsequently, I'd be given Herceptin every three weeks for a year. I was heartened to hear that there was such a drug. I opted to have twelve weekly rounds of chemo first, then surgery and radiation. I couldn't wait to get started and made the very conscious decision to leave fear behind. What good was it going to do me? I loved my busy, rich, full life way too much to waste any time on anxious thoughts. Positivity would be my modus operandi for the foreseeable future. I was going to beat this thing, no question.

So there I was in mid-February 2023, with my chemotherapy, surgery, and radiation all done but still going to the Princess Margaret Cancer Centre every three weeks for my Herceptin. It might sound crazy, but my regular visits were something I actually looked forward to. The hospital staff were all so kind and caring, and I knew this place would heal me. There was so very much to be grateful for.

Iain and I had celebrated Valentine's Day the evening before with a very romantic dinner, and he was accompanying me—as he almost always did—to get my Herceptin infusion in one of the chemotherapy pods. I was wearing my trusty silver cuff, as usual, but I took it off to receive my treatment, plopping it down beside me on the chemo bed. My wonderful nurse, Rosie, got my vein ready for the impending infusion and brought me one of those brilliantly comforting warm flannel blankets to cozy up with—always a big treat for patients visiting those chemo pods.

When the infusion was over, I got up, and Iain and I went right home. But shortly after I arrived, I looked down at my wrist and realized my cuff was missing. I knew I had left it in that chemo pod. But no worries. I was sure Rosie or one of the other nurses had found it. I called right away.

"Hi! I just had treatment in the purple pod"—all pods are identified by colors—"and I left a silver cuff bracelet there," I told the nurse who answered the phone. "Have you found it?"

"I haven't seen anything, but wait a minute, I'll go check," she told me.

A couple of minutes later, she was back with the worrisome news. "Sorry, nothing like that has turned up. But we'll call you if it does."

My heart sank. I knew it was only a material possession—but it felt so emblematic of my power. I tried calling several more times over the next couple of days, but to no avail. My "Wonder Woman" cuff was gone. Vanished. Just like that—after a quarter of a century on my wrist! The nurses had likely sent all the bedding to the laundry with the cuff folded up in the sheets.

"People have lost watches, even dentures!" one nurse told me. *C'est la vie,* I thought.

It took me some time, but eventually, I just had to let it go. I was not going to find that cuff ever again, and it was a waste of energy to be sad about it. Instead, I tried to think about this loss in a positive, meaningful way. That piece of jewelry had served me so well for so many years. And maybe I'd lost it because I didn't really need it anymore. My treatment had gone well, and I was healing. And maybe that cuff hadn't actually been the source of my power after all. Maybe the power had been inside me all along.

Sometimes I like to think about where that silver cuff ended up. Maybe it has moved on to someone else who needs it more than I do right now. Maybe it's helping someone else reclaim their power and feel like Wonder Woman. Wherever it is, and whoever is wearing it, I wish them health, strength, and courage.

Cool Is a State of Mind

While fashion statements in black and white have always been among the most elegant to me, there's one eighties ensemble I wore that took on a significance I never could have imagined at the time. I wore it for an encounter with one of rock's most colorful icons, Keith Richards.

It all started earnestly enough: In search of attention and credibility, a group of talented Canadian designers based in Toronto formed a coalition called TOD—which stood for Toronto Ontario Designers. As a way of promoting their wares, they asked to dress me. At the time, I was not only contributing to Citytv's music programming and *MuchMusic*, I was also hosting *Fashion Television*, so I was getting all kinds of on- and off-air exposure. It was a welcome opportunity for me to promote Canadian designers and to explore a diverse range of looks.

One of the TOD designers was Shelly Walsh, a young talent who'd apprenticed at the Emilio Pucci fashion house in Florence before returning to Toronto to represent a European design firm. She launched her first spring collection in 1985 to rave reviews. She gave me one of the easy-to-wear outfits from that collection to sport on the air: a three-piece pantsuit ensemble, featuring unconventional, playful polka dots and stripes in classic black and white. Though it was far from avant-garde, I welcomed the whimsy of this casual, chic outfit—a far cry from many of the conservative looks that Canadian designers were presenting at the time.

When I was invited by CBS Records to fly to Antigua for an interview with Keith Richards, I excitedly packed the new outfit, confident it would give me the edge required for a meeting with the rock legend. The Stones had just come out with their eighteenth British and twentieth American studio album—their first under their new contract with Columbia Records. According to accounts, the album had been recorded during a time when Keith Richards and Mick Jagger's relationship had gone off the rails a bit. There'd been reports that Keith and Mick had been fighting over the band's direction.

The beach at Antigua's majestic St. James Hotel was as close to heaven as I could imagine. With its turquoise water and white, sandy beach, it was a picture-perfect postcard setting for our interview. Keith was quite passionate about this Caribbean island, where he regularly vacationed with his beautiful wife, Patti Hansen, so I understood why he had opted for this paradise for our chat. Also, Patti was pregnant with their second child at the time. Why not just kick back with his wife and baby, and await the arrival of baby number two in a perfect setting?

I was eager to capture Keith in all his relaxed glory, intent on finding out how he was managing to strike a balance between work and life. Was he satisfied with his accomplishments—personally, professionally, and artistically?

It was decided that our interview would take place on a dock down by the beach. I realized then that the black-and-white ensemble I'd planned on wearing might not fit the bill, so I opted for a pale blue denim miniskirt with an oversized light blue denim shirt thrown over a black tank top. I accompanied this with a pair of white ballet flats and plastic star earrings for an extra bit of fun. The look certainly didn't scream "fashion" or "edge," but I hoped the ultracasual style suggested I was confident and relaxed rather than trying too hard. (The truth was more complicated, of course—I was about to interview a real-life Rolling Stone—and arguably the coolest one at that. I'll admit I was a little bit nervous!)

From the moment I laid eyes on Keith, I knew he was every bit the authentic rock and roller he was cracked up to be. A little shy but incredibly warm, he used his cigarette as a prop, punctuating his thoughts with deep drags. The lean, suntanned Keith exuded his own powerful brand of sex appeal, clad in a pair of casual white cotton trousers and a black three-button pullover jersey, sleeves pushed to his elbows. He had a pair of well-worn white sneakers on his feet and his signature silver skull ring on his right middle finger. I couldn't wait to sit down with him.

Our conversation started amicably enough, with me commenting on how wonderful I found the vibe in Antigua and Keith telling me what great taste his wife had in island-hopping.

"You're in incredible shape, or so it seems," I told him. "Is that something you've been working on? Getting in shape on purpose?"

"No, it's pretty much the same shape I'm always in," he said with a smile, almost embarrassed. His humility was endearing and completely sincere. "I've just got more sun on it," he said with a laugh.

After that, I got down to business. I knew die-hard Stones fans were worried about the news that had surfaced earlier that week. The word was that Mick wasn't all that enamored with the *Dirty Work* album, which had just been released. Apparently he'd sent a telegram to Keith telling him to forget about going on tour because the album wasn't worth it. Rolling Stone devotees wondered if this might be heralding the breakup of the band. But when I asked Keith about the rumor, he could not have been more diplomatic.

He took another deep drag of his cigarette. "I mean, I've received quite a few cables and letters from Mick. You know it's hard just to call each other when the phone service isn't what it should be. But no, basically, we're going to get together in London a couple of weeks from now to shoot a new video. And I suppose there won't be a big tour this summer. When I get back, we'll find out if we'll do something in the fall. But it's just a matter of timing, really. Everybody's doing this, doing that. We're just trying to slot it all in."

I knew how passionate Keith was about playing live, and it seemed to me like Mick was calling the shots.

"Do you end up resenting it?" I asked. "Because I know how much you love performing."

"Yeah . . . Like, not so much resentment. I'm just a pretty self-ish guy. I like to play with the Stones. You know, I'm one of those guys who goes, 'Come on, you guys, let's go!' But everybody's gotta want to do it. So . . . we'll find out."

Our conversation went on to the importance of doing videos in this new age of music consumption. Keith astutely noted that "TV and rock 'n' roll got married." He then predicted that music videos were going to turn into their own form of entertainment and not necessarily be tied to the release of a record.

We also talked about the blues and what an important influence that genre had been on him. And then we moved on to Keith's creative drive and what keeps him and the Stones going.

"We're still looking for the Stones, in a way," he reflected. "We still don't think we've really found it. I mean, maybe that's just something that we use to keep it all going, you know what I mean? In other words, we're not totally satisfied that we've actually got the ultimate Rolling Stones down. So I guess it's sort of a search for that."

I was blown away by the candor and humility of this state-ment. After all of his success, Keith was still interested in improvement.

"It must be really hard to maintain an edge when superfi-cially, anyway, on so many levels, everything seems so perfect. I mean, where does that hunger come from?" I asked.

"It's not so much about trying to be creatively new or different. Creative edge comes from behind. . . . It's kind of like somebody's behind you, chasing you with an ax. You try and do the best you can, and you hope it comes out great. But even if it doesn't, don't let it be a bummer. I think it's just more of a push. You don't want to blow it."

There was more talk about Keith's creative process with Mick, the way his family helped him balance his lifestyle, and the fear and paranoia he used to have—especially when it came to cops. But these days, he told me, he refused to live his life always looking over his shoulder.

There was something else I wanted to explore. "Does it surprise you," I asked, "that it all works, the longevity of the Stones . . . that staying power of your music?"

"In the days when we started, nobody lasted more than two years maximum. When our first record came out, we all looked at each other, and said, 'Oh no! It's the beginning of the end, man!'" He laughed then. "So, in that way, we were surprised. But I got used to it now."

"People have said that if Jagger is the heart of the Rolling Stones, you're certainly the soul. Do you feel personally responsible for keeping the band together?"

"I don't really feel that I do any more than anybody else. I just want my little patch of it. For me, Charlie Watts is as much the soul of the Stones as anybody. I mean, I take my hat off there. . . . I just jostle them up a bit in the studio, and try and organize sounds. Otherwise, everybody keeps everybody else going. It's an amazing collection of people. God knows why it works."

By the time we wrapped our interview, I was totally besotted with this warm, sensitive, and soft-spoken guy who oozed cool. I was so in awe of how he managed to keep his feet on the ground and remain a loving family man in a ruthless business rife with egomaniacs.

Keith was kind and generous with his time, and the next day, just before my cameraman and I made our way to the airport, he popped by our hotel to say goodbye. He was dressed in a dark blue shirt, looking a little edgier than he had on that sunny beach the day before. I had on the black-and-white striped and polka-dotted outfit I hadn't yet had the chance to wear.

Keith casually put his arm around me, and we posed for a photo, all smiles for the camera. The result was a truly memorable shot, with Keith's famous skull ring in full view on the hand slung around my shoulder.

Back home in Toronto, still giddy over the wonderful encounter I'd had with Keith, I got the photo developed and had it framed for display in my living room. I still look at it from time to time and wonder how I, a kid who grew up freaking out over how impossibly hip the Stones were when their *High Tide and Green Grass* album came out, actually managed to meet Keith Richards twenty years later! I couldn't have dreamed of anything cooler.

But show business is a roller coaster. A couple of months later, that same black-and-white, polka-dots-and-stripes outfit I wore in the picture with Keith Richards sent me into a tailspin. I was innocently leafing through the new issue of a high-profile Canadian women's magazine when I stumbled upon their "worst dressed" list. And there I was, making the list because of my Shelly Walsh outfit.

Suddenly, I felt diminished and small. I was mortified to have been called out in this way! But what I really couldn't understand was why I was being picked on for supporting a Canadian designer! Wasn't this magazine supposed to be celebrating Canadian fashion rather than dissing it?

I licked my wounds over the next few days, and eventually, I came to an important realization: So what if the powers that be at a magazine thought I was one of my country's worst dressed? I knew who I was, and there was no accounting for taste. If they didn't like it, they could lump it! Besides, that same outfit had been immortalized in a photo alongside one of the coolest rock stars on the planet! I decided this magazine's criticism was something I could live with—or better yet, walk away from.

Now, as I look back on the moment, I no longer feel any shame at all. To this day, that photo of Keith and me in my "worst dressed" outfit sits proudly on my piano, a constant reminder that no matter how you dress, cool is ultimately a state of mind.

I can't help but recall Keith's wise words on the beach that day: "You try and do the best you can, and you hope it comes out great. But even if it doesn't, don't let it be a bummer."

The Amazing Technicolor
Dream Jacket

When it comes to flashy standouts in my wardrobe stash, few things can compare with my rainbow-striped, hand-dyed silk jacket, not only because it was custom-made for me but also because it marked a kind of coming-of-age. The mandarin-style jacket, which I acquired in early 1983, came directly from a Queen Street West artisan's studio. But sadly—and embarrassingly—I can't for the life of me remember the name of the talented artist who created it. Still, it has become a very important garment to me.

The first time I wore it was for my inaugural newspaper profile shoot. The late Peter Goddard, who was the *Toronto Star*'s pop critic at the time, was writing a piece about me for the *Star*'s entertainment section. Although Peter had always been very kind and respectful towards me, many other Toronto journalists were not so favorable.

"Who is that big-mouthed, big-nosed gal with the irritating voice?" they'd ask—perhaps not always in so many words, but trust me, that was the common sentiment about me in those days—and I knew it. Some journalists didn't believe I had any business rubbing shoulders with famous rock stars and reporting on them. I was too brash and in-yer-face and personal for the "serious" music journalism they craved. I'm sure many of them felt I'd gotten the job without paying my dues.

But the interview with Peter and the photo shoot that went along with it on the front page of the *Star*'s popular Saturday entertainment section in April 1983 marked a turning point of sorts. Not that everyone was convinced I was finally doing great work—but for the city's largest newspaper to be devoting that much space and ink to me—well, maybe I was doing something right after all.

As soon as I read the headline, I felt empowered and emboldened: "How Jeanne Mixes Pop and Chutzpah." There I was, a defiant look on my face and clad in my loud, multicolored silk jacket, thrown over a bright red spandex unitard and little black miniskirt. I hadn't realized at the time, but clutching my open jacket with both fists was as if I'd taken on the stance of a heavyweight fighter. The only thing missing was a pair of boxing gloves.

"Jeanne Beker has these awful dreams," wrote Peter. "They're about everyone hating her—everyone. They don't like her clothes.

They don't like her mouth. They don't like her hair. They don't like what she says, how she says it, why she says it, or when she says it. It's awful, awful, awful. She'll jolt awake feeling terrible. 'What have I ever done?' she'll wonder.'"

That's what Peter wrote, right off the top. He exposed me for all my vulnerabilities. It may not have been the way I would have chosen for the piece to begin, but I cannot deny that it got people's attention.

I called my parents as soon as I received the paper, knowing a copy had also been delivered to their home. How would they feel about this big splash of publicity about their daughter?

"Oy, mazel tov! That's some big picture," my mum kvelled the second she picked up the phone. "And they say you mix pop and chutzpah?" She laughed. "Well, good for you."

I knew my parents didn't love all the revelations in the piece, but at least Mum was happy that a Yiddish word appeared in the headline.

Peter went on to reveal that the publicity brochure for *The NewMusic*—the show I was cohosting with J. D. Roberts—described me as an "entertainment reporter." "And it's here where you discover something truly is amiss," wrote Peter. "This is tantamount to describing a lightning bolt as a little bit of static."

Citytv's revered president, Moses Znaimer, was also interviewed for the feature. He'd shown me tough love in the past, giving me both incredible opportunities and a number of very rough rides, but I was pleased that, in print, he was singing my praises. Not surprisingly, my close buddy Toller Cranston had also chimed in favorably.

As I sat at the breakfast table with my coffee, poring over the article for about the fifth time, an unparalleled feeling of satisfaction and pride swelled up in me. I'd done it. I'd survived the slings and arrows of cynical detractors and made my career path on my own terms. And as for that wonderful "jacket of many colors" I'd chosen to wear for that photo shoot, it might have seemed like an absurd fashion choice, even a foolish one to some. But not to me. That's how it is sometimes: Fashion has a magical way of revealing the inner truth and reflecting it outwardly for everyone to see—colorfully, uniquely, boldly.

Canoeing with Kate Moss

While I've had the privilege of rubbing shoulders with some of the world's most glamorous style cognoscenti over the years, it's usually been on their own turf: at fashion shows, design studios, photo shoots, and chic social gatherings. So when I found myself paddling a canoe on Ontario's idyllic Gull Lake on the first day of fall in 2017 with one of the world's most celebrated and beloved models, it was a real "pinch me" moment. It's because of this moment that a certain unassuming, polyester print top from my very own eponymous clothing line will always hold a special place in my wardrobe. On that morning, I'd teamed it with my favorite old pair of denim jeans, creating a casual, relaxed look that was perfect for the cottage and, as it turned out, totally fine for hanging out with the iconic Kate Moss.

I'd first met Kate in the spring of 1990, when she was nineteen, for a *Cosmopolitan* magazine cover shoot. This was at the Manhattan studio of the late photographer Francesco Scavullo. *Cosmo* was famous for featuring voluptuous, ultraglam cover girls, and the up-and-coming Kate seemed an unlikely subject at the time. She showed up to the shoot in a teeny, grungy kids' sweater, schleppy bell-bottoms, and nerdy running shoes. She had an old chiffon scarf tied around her neck, and her hair was messily piled atop her head. Hers was a thrift-shop look, ahead of its time, you might say, and the kind of style concoction only a gorgeous young model like Kate could pull off. As "unstylish" as I thought she looked at the time, I knew her antifashion statement would probably become the next big thing. And so it did a couple of seasons later.

In person, Kate was laid-back and quiet—almost a little shy. I felt bad for her when Scavullo's stylist had major problems pinning her into a sexy top and taping her boobs to give her cleavage. But this was a model who rolled with the punches, and within a couple of years, Kate was a certifiable supermodel, famous for her waif-like look and unique proportions (only five-foot-seven in a world where most models were at least five-ten).

As I got to know her through the years during our backstage encounters, Kate never failed to delight me. She was quick-witted, always one to voice clever quips. She laughed wholeheartedly and was outspoken in her opinions. I remember her being irate when there were some media rumblings that her skinny build promoted anorexia, in spite of the fact that it was her natural body type. I interviewed Kate and famed makeup artist Kevyn Aucoin backstage in New York about the controversy, and both were pretty frustrated by the injustice of the accusation.

"People should start taking responsibility for the choices they make instead of blaming Kate Moss because they want to look thin," Kevyn insisted.

"Exactly! Exactly!" chimed in Kate. "Thank you!"

"That's not her responsibility," continued Kevyn. "Go to a therapist, honey."

"It's true," said Kate, obviously grateful to Kevyn for coming to her defense.

There was no question that life in the fashion spotlight was rife with pressures, but no matter what predicament she found herself in, Kate always managed to rise above the noise, retaining the respect of clients and fans alike. I took pleasure in watching her star rise and often thought of her as simply the best—arguably the most influential and controversial model of her time.

In 2016, Kate added another impressive feather to her professional cap when she was named the face of Decorté, an established Japanese luxury skincare brand. She came to Toronto for the brand's Canadian launch, and we were reunited in a back room at Saks Fifth Avenue's downtown store for an interview for *The Globe and Mail*. *Fashion Television* had gone off the air about four years before that, so it had been a while since we'd seen each other.

"Oh my god! I can't believe it's you!" Kate squealed when she laid eyes on me.

I was thrilled to see this bright light in my own hometown.

We reminisced about the past and especially about the first time I'd met her, how she'd seemed so shy.

"I know there may have been a lot of insecurity at first," I said.

"Yeah . . . shy . . ." she admitted wistfully.

I said that she always seemed solid, too, like she knew who she was.

"I think I just felt really lucky that I wasn't in Croydon, where I grew up," she replied. "So I thought that even if everything goes horribly wrong, I'm not losing anything. . . . I was just always having fun."

"You certainly never had any attitude either," I told her. "Every photographer I've ever interviewed about you, every designer who's looked at you as a muse, every editor . . . they all just love working with you. It speaks volumes about your professionalism and the way you see the business."

"I mean I get that it's work and I want to get the picture. I'm a perfectionist in a way. I would never leave a job at five because that's the time I can leave. I stay to make sure that it's perfect, because I want to do the best job, really."

Kate's humble attitude was incredibly refreshing. She went on to tell me that every season she wondered if she was ever going to get another job. I told her it was wonderful to see how she'd maintained that humility when she'd been lionized to such a degree.

"I don't really listen to that," she said matter-of-factly.

"What about your idea of beauty? How has that changed over the years?"

"I've always thought that beautiful people are the people with character, who are beautiful from the inside. Characters are really beautiful to me because I've been surrounded by models all my life, and sometimes they're not the beautiful people, even when they look pretty. So the characters are the ones I love."

We spent the rest of our time together talking about how lucky we were to have experienced fashion's "Golden Age" and how the business just wasn't the same anymore. By the end of the conversation, Kate and I were dreaming about the possibility of working on a project together—a documentary that would chronicle the good old days in the fashion scene.

"Well, if anybody's gonna tell that story, it should be us!" Kate said with a laugh.

"What a fantasy that would be! I'm going to see what's possible," I replied.

Kate's business partner, Lucy Baxter, gave me her number and told me to keep in touch.

In the months that followed, I started seriously toying with the idea of producing a documentary with Kate based on the wonderful old material in the *Fashion Television* archives. But since I didn't really have a relationship with the new players at Bell Media, I would need help getting access. My dear friend Jeffrey Latimer, an entertainment impresario with some great connections to the new management, said he'd be happy to assist. Perhaps we could interest Kate in coming to Toronto and screening some of the precious old footage? That would certainly help fuel our documentary dream, and it would show Bell Media that we had a major talent on side.

A few weeks later, I was pinching myself yet again, because I was having a fabulous, champagne-drenched oyster lunch at

London's Soho House with Jeffrey, Kate, and Lucy Baxter. I was trying hard to coax Kate to come to Canada.

"I'll go," she said, "but only if we can have an authentic Canadian experience. I'd really love to see a bear," she said with a laugh.

"Well, not sure we can arrange that," said Jeffrey. "But my family has a rustic old cottage on a lake outside of Toronto. We could spend some time there."

I could see in Kate's eyes that she was seriously considering this, so I took up my phone and dialed my friend Izzy Sulejmani, who owns a fabulous photography gallery in Toronto. He was a huge fan, and I knew he wanted to host a kind of retrospective of Kate's work over the years by some of the fashion world's top photographers. Maybe this would add appeal to our request.

"Izzy," I said when he picked up. "I'm here with Kate Moss, and I believe you wanted to ask her something."

I turned the phone over to Kate.

"Izzy!" she squealed. "How great to talk to you."

Kate had briefly met Izzy on a previous trip to Toronto, and the two had gotten on famously.

I waited impatiently as Kate listened to Izzy, nodding her head from time to time.

Finally, she said the words I most wanted to hear—"It's a deal! Let's do it!"

Jeffrey and I could barely contain our excitement. Kate was coming to Toronto—and for a visit at Jeffrey's family's cottage to boot. We were giddy as we hugged goodbye, looking forward to what promised to be an incredible weekend.

Izzy's gallery show was arranged for September. Kate and I

would spend the day at Bell Media screening old tapes before the gallery party. But leading up to it all, Kate and Lucy would fly from Toronto to Jeffrey's family cottage in a private plane. My partner, Iain, and I would drive to the lake and meet the others when they got there. What I hadn't realized was that the evening Kate was coming was Erev Rosh Hashanah—the first night of the Jewish New Year. I determined then and there to serve a proper Jewish holiday dinner.

When the night arrived and we were all gathered around the table, Kate's eyes lit up as I blessed the holiday candles and explained the significance of eating apples and honey for a sweet year ahead. She couldn't have been more respectful and intrigued, and I was incredibly moved to be sharing my precious religious traditions with her and Lucy.

We spent the evening curled up in front of the big fireplace, watching *Fashion Television*'s twenty-fifth anniversary special, and it felt as though we were one big family. The next day was spent lazing around the dock in the sunshine. Iain and I had to leave a bit early. I went inside to change into jeans and my favorite old Edit by Jeanne Beker brand polyester top. "I'd love to go for a canoe ride before we leave," I told Jeffrey.

"Oh, I'd love to go with you!" chimed in Kate.

Tout de suite, Jeffrey got a canoe out, gave us a couple of paddles, and told us to "go out there and create something fabulous together!"

I gingerly stepped into the canoe, taking the stern position. I doubted Kate had ever been in a canoe before, and she certainly had never steered one. And so we took off, Kate nursing a flute of champagne in one hand, cigarette in the other, and me, trying my best to navigate. It felt like we were in some kind of exotic *Vogue* editorial spread, but it also was so casual and friendly.

We indulged in cozy conversation, talking about everything from our kids to our love lives. I was blown away by her candor, good humor, and lighthearted positivity. I adored her for all of it.

In the end, our big documentary project never came to be—or at least it hasn't happened yet—but I truly cherish the photos Iain took from the dock that weekend. My favorite is of Kate and me in the canoe. There I am, sporting my cheap and cheerful polyester "Jeanne Beker" top, chauffeuring one of the world's hottest high-fashion models in an old canoe on a sparkling Canadian lake. Anything really is possible in this magical life—the proof is in the picture.

Tartan Ties

The longing for joyful and meaningful family ties has always been with me—likely because our family was so small—and I've often envied those with dozens of aunts and uncles and cousins who share not only bloodlines but histories. That's why a chic purple-and-green tartan coat that lives in my closet has taken on such meaning for me and is one treasured gift I'll never part with.

That first, magical night that my partner, Iain, came into my life, he, too, must have known we were in for something good. So perhaps it isn't any wonder that he asked me if I'd consider going to his native Scotland with him. He'd immigrated to Canada with his family when he was about eleven years old and went back to Scotland rather regularly. But although he'd been through two rather lengthy marriages before we got together, neither of his wives was ever inclined to accompany him to his beloved homeland.

When Iain sent me that irresistible invitation the night we met, and I immediately accepted, little did I know that not only would I be embarking on a wonderfully memorable trip to an inspiring part of the world but I'd also be connecting with extraordinary people who were about to become integral parts of my family.

"Just wait till you meet Uncle Alasdair!" Iain enthused on the plane to Glasgow. "He's so amazing. And Aunt Angela is just the sweetest. They're going to love you!"

As excited as I was to meet Iain's favorite uncle and aunt, I was a bit leery of how they might react to me. After all, we'd only met a couple of months earlier. Still, we were madly in love. Iain had no qualms about his relatives' reactions. "They're just going to be happy for us," he assured me. "You'll see."

The youngest brother of Iain's late mother, Alasdair Gillies, and his lovely wife, Angela, live in a small village outside of Glasgow, in a fairy tale home called "The Heath" on a couple of lush green acres boasting magnificent gardens, thanks to Angela's green thumb. Angela is also an expert baker, and her productive country kitchen is always stocked with biscuit tins filled with "Melting Moments" cookies and her delicious oaties, both sweet and savory. She's also a lover of fashion and has an impressive little stash of cherished, decades-old wardrobe pieces made of the finest Harris Tweed and mohair fabrics.

Now in their eighties, the elegant couple are the picture of charm and class. Alasdair's larger-than-life personality and boyish charisma is intensely endearing. A retired dentist who spent a decade in Riyadh practicing at a military hospital, Alasdair had had an early career in music. Born on the Isle of Skye, he was one of Scotland's most famous Gaelic singers, having started singing professionally at the age of seven, and even having once hosted a Canadian TV show called *Ceilidh* in the seventies. A strapping, handsome performer, not only was he a personable presenter but he gave new meaning to the sex appeal of kilts. In recent years, he had been appointed an MBE (Member of the Order of the British Empire) by Queen Elizabeth for his philanthropic work and his contributions to Gaelic culture. And while I was blown away when Iain first told me about his uncle's illustrious achievements, when I actually got to meet the man and experience firsthand that radiant twinkle in his sky-blue eyes, I was instantly smitten.

"Well, hello, Jeanne!" Alasdair roared the morning he met us at the Glasgow Airport. "We're thrilled Sean has brought you to Scotland!"

Since his childhood, all of Iain's relatives have called him Sean, because his father was also named Iain, and Sean is Irish Gaelic for Ian. The change in name avoided confusion and suited him perfectly, since he's a huge fan of Sean Connery.

"Angela's prepared a big breakfast for you two, so let's go straight back to the house. It's going to be a busy few days," Alasdair said with a smile. "And we're just so happy to have you stay with us."

The long driveway to Alasdair and Angela's home was lined with magnificent fuchsia rhododendrons, and the striking white stucco house that finally appeared was as welcoming as it was pic-

turesque. Angela was waiting on the doorstep, a trim and diminutive lady decked out in a pretty apron. Shoulder-length gray
tresses were held back from her face with a hair band. Her smile
couldn't have been sweeter, and in that lovely Scottish accent, she
invited Iain and me into the house and gave us both big hugs.

"I've got some fresh eggs and a little black pudding prepared
for you," she said. "So come into the dining room and let's have a
cup of tea." Immediately, it felt as though she couldn't do enough
for us. As I made my way through the house, I was charmed by
the wall-to-wall plaid carpeting. We were in Scotland all right,
embraced by the friendliest and most loving pair imaginable. As
Sean reached for my hand and led me into the house, I couldn't
have felt happier.

That evening, we sat in the back-room conservatory sipping
on our wee drams of Scotch and gazing out at the dramatically
lit back garden, where a majestic fox prowled about. Watching it
made for great entertainment. And if that wasn't enough, Alasdair regaled us with stories about his days working with the royal
family in Saudi Arabia.

At the end of the evening, Iain and I retired to our room,
feeling exhausted but content. The next morning, as I sauntered
downstairs for breakfast, I suddenly heard a familiar old song.

"*I dream of Jeanie with the light brown hair . . .*" Someone was
singing in a sweet, booming voice, and it was a song I recognized
instantly, an old Stephen Foster tune my parents always playfully
sang to me when I was a child. And as I stepped off the bottom
stair and turned the corner, the brightly grinning Uncle Alasdair
came into view, half-laughing at my surprise and delight. For a

second I believed Alasdair himself was serenading me, but I soon realized the tune was coming from a CD he'd recorded years ago, one of the many spirited albums he has to his credit.

"That takes me right back!" I squealed. "I haven't heard that song for decades. And what a fantastic rendition."

"It's the least I could do for you, Jeanne," said Alasdair with a hearty laugh. "Just wanted to make you feel as welcome as possible."

"Oh, you've done that all right. I may never want to leave!"

Iain watched our exchange from a distance, pleased that his charming Scottish relatives were making such a wonderful impression on me.

"Aunt Angela's arranged a fun and thoughtful outing for us this afternoon," Iain announced. "We've been invited to drop by the showroom of one of Glasgow's most popular designers."

"That's right," called Angela from the kitchen. "Joyce Young is having a little champagne reception at her renovated new location, and we're all going!"

All this and fashion, too? It seemed too good to be true. I couldn't wait to meet Joyce and check out her collection. Apparently, this talented designer was a favorite of Iain's first cousin Fiona Kennedy, the much-loved Aberdeen-based singer. And though I hadn't yet met the beautiful Fiona, I'd heard she was a woman of great style. My appetite for a wee Scottish fashion fix had definitely been whetted.

The building we pulled up to that afternoon was on Maryhill Road. It seemed a little lackluster from the outside—a boxy, very minimal modern structure that hardly looked like it could house any kind of fashion emporium. But the moment we walked through the front door, we were transported. The beautifully appointed, richly carpeted space, with its elegant décor, fine furnishings, and enchanting vibe, was as chic as any showroom I'd been to in the world's fashion capitals. I knew I'd come to a spot where good taste abounded.

Joyce Young and her husband, Maurice, were a lovely couple, and champagne in hand, I was taken on a tour of the premises, which boasted a busy workroom, separate bridal salon, and luxe dressing rooms. Of course it was the actual goods that I was fascinated with—and those included endless bolts of some of the most exquisite tartan fabrics imaginable.

While the last thing I needed was another frock, I couldn't resist diving into the racks of fabulous fashions. As I was browsing through the eclectic pieces, while Iain and Alasdair and Angela patiently stood by, one garment stopped me in my tracks: a vibrant purple-and-green tartan coat, with dolman sleeves and emerald detachable faux-fur trim on the collar and cuffs. The unusual color combination was delectable, and I knew I had to try the piece on.

The designer herself was the first to comment. "Oh, that is really fab on you! Suits you perfectly."

"I absolutely adore this coat," I enthused. It was understated and easy, classic yet a tad whimsical for such a finely tailored garment.

Iain walked over to take a closer look. "It really is you, babe," he said, and then turning to Joyce, he gave a nod. "We'll take it!"

Iain bought the coat just like that. I was floored by his generosity and especially taken with the fact that in all my sixty-three years, no boyfriend had ever bought me a precious garment like this before. Scarves, lingerie, and even silk pajamas . . . but a stunning wool coat? And a tartan one at that? It was wildly romantic, and I loved him for it. The fact that this coat was by a designer from Glasgow made it even more meaningful.

"Ah, such a bonnie lass," Iain whispered to me as I wore the new coat on the way back to Alasdair and Angela's. I felt so proud strutting in purple tartan, and though the coat was inspired by a different cultural backdrop from my own, somehow, it and everything in Scotland felt so familiar to me.

The next day, laughter rang out in the kitchen at The Heath as dear Aunt Angela taught me how to make her famous oaties, always using a heart-shaped cookie cutter, of course. It's an easy recipe and one I adore, and there's something comforting about the taste of these simple, traditional biscuits. These days I bake at least one batch of oaties a week, to remind myself of that special home away from home. And you can just imagine what donning that purple-and-green tartan coat does for me! It was the perfect souvenir of a most memorable trip to Scotland, and a stylish reminder that precious family ties sometimes come in the sweetest and most unexpected ways.

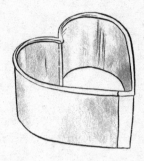

Aunt Angela's Oaties

Cream together:

8 oz. butter or margarine

4 oz. sugar

1 pinch salt

Add:

1 cup flour

3 cups porridge oats or quick oats

Mix well and roll out to desired thickness.

Then cut into shapes.

(The mixture will be sticky, so use flour on your rolling pin!)

Bake at 350 for 17 to 20 minutes.

EPILOGUE

I hope you've enjoyed this wistful wander through my personal wardrobe of memory. In many ways, it's you who have inspired this book. So often when I meet people familiar with me and my career, they ask how many closets I have, and I sometimes think they're not actually wondering about how much real estate I devote to my clothing but about my very deepest self and how that's reflected through my clothing choices. This curiosity speaks to how what we wear defines us and how fashion reflects who we are at various times in our lives.

As for my closet space, it is now something I think about less literally. That "space" is populated with so many good memories of what I wore at certain times in my life, and it reflects not only who I was but who I've become. As you know, every fashion collection has a style of its own; this is as true of my wardrobe as it is of yours.

The pieces in this book are my best attempt to share the vivid, colorful, and well-worn life I am lucky to call my own. My travels and my clothing have taken me through so many styles, ages, and stages, and I hope that my recollections have inspired you to think about your own wardrobe with renewed wonder and reverence.

Whether you've hung on to some of those meaningful pieces that were such formative parts of your personal identity, or whether those pieces are now preserved only via photographic images or fond memories, I know that remembering what you wore—why you chose certain garments, how you wore them, the way they made you feel, and how others perceived you in them—is an exercise rooted not only in nostalgia but in self-discovery.

Now, when people ask me how many closets I have, I think of the question in an all-new way—as a limitless vault of memory where I see my style and personality evolve through time. Through memory, I've preserved a life lived in fashion, and it is always ready to wear.

I've been so fortunate to spend a career in fashion's trenches, in the company of many of the world's great designers and fashionistas. I've rubbed shoulders with the most esteemed style cognoscenti, and I've loved every second of it. It would be easy to assume that I've amassed quite a collection of interesting, exotic garments as a result of my work, and while I have, I find myself returning over and over again not to the actual clothing but to the lessons I learned from the people who created those pieces or inspired me to wear them.

Fashion itself may not make the world go round, but far beyond the materialistic aspects of its pursuit, it brings color and attitude to life's big ride. In essence, fashion makes life fun and fabulous. It reminds us our lives are worthy of commemoration and celebration. When we move through the world with style, we cultivate an appreciation of ourselves and others. This spirit of exuberance will never fall out of fashion. This is a life well worn.

ACKNOWLEDGMENTS

While my wardrobe pieces have always served to lift me higher, nothing can compare to the league of beating hearts that have stood by me, supported me, and cheered me on. Huge thanks to Kevin Hanson, who helped plant the seed for this book, believing that I had important life lessons to share; and to the brilliant Nita Pronovost (aka Nita Prose), who helped me fashion this wardrobe of stories, always encouraging me to dig a little deeper.

Thanks to all the outstanding TV producers I've had the privilege of working with, from *The NewMusic* and *MuchMusic*'s late, great John Martin to *Fashion Television*'s Marcia Martin, Jay Levine, Howard Brull, and Mary Benadiba. A special shout-out to the wonderful Christopher Sherman, who not only often took care of me in the trenches but became one of my nearest and dearest confidants in the process. And of course, huge thanks to all those talented cameramen I had the joy of "dancing" with, including Hernan Morris, Patrick Pidgeon, Arthur Pressick, Martin Brown, Jim Needham, Basil Young, Jeff Brinkert, and

Scott Burgess, who were my eyewitnesses to all of the magic. And much gratitude to Jodie Epstein at the Bell Media Archives. Also forever grateful to media visionary Moses Znaimer for having dreamed up the notion of the feisty Citytv in the first place. And thanks to fellow dreamer Michael King for helping me realize so many "glossy" fantasies.

I will forever be indebted to all the fabulous designers I've met along the way, who gave me an even deeper appreciation for the power of fashion and the profound messaging it can convey to others and ourselves. So much gratitude to my TSC family for all the feel-good fun this past decade, especially Natalie Belmont, Liana Vangelisti, Michelle DaSilva, Neeraj Ghai, makeup artist Genny Rovito, and stylist Janielle McCoy. My "Style Matters" series has enabled me to really talk to women "where they live"— and allowed me to be both spirited and pragmatic about fashion's possibilities.

Big shout-out to the ever stylish and hugely philanthropic Suzanne Rogers for all her support and generosity. And a huge thank-you to my agents Melanie Roy at Speakers Spotlight and Lindsey Love and Sundance Filardi of the Spotlight Agency for their efforts on my behalf. Special thanks to the team at Calgary's Glenbow Museum, including Melanie Kjorlien and Nicholas Bell, for the shape of things to come, and Paul Hardy for all the dreaming and scheming.

So grateful to have worked with Simon & Schuster Canada on this book, and especially for my patient editor, Brittany Lavery, who came into the picture at a late but vital stage and took such good care of me, along with Nicole Winstanley, Kaitlyn Lonnee,

Randall Perry, and the top-notch publicity/marketing team of Rita Silva, Cayley Pimentel, and Cali Platek.

My cancer journey proved to be one of the most extraordinary experiences of my life, teaching me myriad lessons about compassion, hope, and positivity. Thank you to all the amazing caregivers, technicians, nurses, and doctors at Toronto's mighty Princess Margaret Cancer Centre, especially Dr. Tulin Cil and Dr. Eitan Amir. And special thanks to Adina Isenberg, who held my hand in those early days, and Miyo Yamashita of the Princess Margaret Foundation, who's convinced me that conquering cancer in our lifetime is a realistic goal.

I have an embarrassment of riches when it comes to inspiring friends, and a complete list is, happily, too long to mention. But here are a few who help ground me and whose perspectives help me remember what's really important in this crazy life: Penny Fiksel, Jackie Feldman, Deenah Mollin, Louise Kennedy, Caroline Kennedy, Melanie Reffes, Diti Dumas, Mary Symons, Vivian Reiss, Freda and Demos Iordanous, Sheree Rasmussen, Gregory Parvatan, Bruce Bailey, Sandra Bernhard, Trevor Born, Stephan Argent, Carl Lyons, Greg Wyard, Chabela and George Ayoub, Bernie and Tim Moore, Kerri and Haig Oundjian, Jaleh Farhadpour and Tom Phillips, Jackson Thurling and Randy Pearle, Dana Sinclair and Jim Sleeth, Jeffrey Latimer, Beth Coyne and Jules Spicer, Tina Moorey and Susan Clarke, Sue Brunt, Bonnie Brooks, Sandy Kybartas, Andrée Gagné, Kate Alexander Daniels, Dawna Treibicz, Heather Mallins, Mark LaBelle, Jennifer Lipkowitz, Lolitta Dandoy, Tammy Leung, Shannon Passero, Fred Howard, and Jaymz Bee.

ACKNOWLEDGMENTS

Huge thanks, too, to my Instagram followers for all the love and support they constantly send my way. They proved to be the wind beneath my wings during a most trying time in my life, and while it might sound a little lofty, their compassion and generosity has really renewed my faith in humanity. I so appreciate them all.

Finally, a thousand thank-yous to my family for always being there for me: My beloved partner, Iain MacInnes, and his beautiful daughters Caitlin, Julie, and Courtney; my incredible sister, Marilyn Beker and my cool brother-in-law, Greg Rorabaugh; my two precious daughters Bekky O'Neil and Joey O'Neil; and my late parents, Bronia and Joseph Beker, who continue to protect and guide me every step of the way. I love them all more than words can say.